ORDER MY STEPS

*Four Biblical Keys to Effective
Decision Making*

By Brenda J. Robinson

Diligence Publishing Company
Bloomfield, New Jersey

Order My Steps
Four Biblical Keys to Effective Decision Making

DEDICATION

This book is dedicated to individuals who desire to make better choices in life in order to gain a greater sense of achievement, peace, joy and fulfillment in their lives.

To my mother, Ada M. Robinson, whose constant love and support overwhelms my heart.

In memory of my beloved father, Bishop Kenneth O. Robinson, Sr., whose life and legacy have exemplified the blessings in allowing God to order one's steps.

TABLE OF CONTENTS

FOREWORD

Brenda Robinson's book entitled *Order My Steps* is an important Christian instructional blueprint, written for anyone who is interested in understanding how to make wiser decisions, to positively impact one's life.

This book, organized by four practical steps, highlights the importance of surrendering to a process of trust, walking in faith, practicing a daily connection with God and surrendering to the promises of God. The transformational wisdom derived from these Biblical principles, reveals a foundation for a belief system that leads to discernment for making right choices.

Understanding the basis of our belief system is important, because it conveys a deeply rooted conviction for what is true and the core principles used to guide our lives. What is true for you?

Why is the book socially relevant today?

As human beings, we have free will, to use any source or type of information to influence our decisions. At times, the decision may be good, yet still recognizing other possibilities could have been better. Then, there are other times when we might ask ourselves, *"What was I thinking? What did I miss? How did I get here?"*

According to Brenda Robinson, we do not have to second guess our decisions, if we accept our true and profound partnership with God. Thus, whenever there is a decision to be made, we must first pray and seek what is God's will for any answer to our questions. According to Romans 12:2 NIV, *Do not conform to the patterns of this world, but be transformed by the renewing of your mind. Then you will be able to test and approve what God's will is- his good, pleasing and perfect will.* In other words, do not follow the flesh, public opinion or the problems of this world when you are trying to make decisions. Seek God first to transform the way of your thinking so that you will know what God's will is for you.

In this timely book, Brenda Robinson shares her personal testimony about a life-long journey on how surrendering to God's call for her life has led to quality choices in making decisions. Her passion for writing this book, is through the lens of being raised by her father Bishop Kenneth O. Robinson, Sr., her educational and professional training as a minister, school and bereavement counselor and now more recently a graduate student at New York Theological Seminary.

The ultimate goal of *Order My Steps* is to make this blueprint as a go-to source for anyone who is seeking to make wiser decisions to demonstrate a higher quality of life.

Anita Underwood, PhD
Nyack College
Dean of Business and Leadership

ACKNOWLEDGEMENTS

I wish to thank God for endowing me with power, wisdom and inspiration to write this book.

My family, thank you for your constant encouragement and support in all my endeavors. I love you!

Elizabeth Stankiewicz, Miriam Desrosiers and Allie Brown, thank you for taking the time to edit my drafts. I appreciate you dearly.

Rev. Gilbert Picket, Sr., my pastor, thank you for your encouragement and support in this project.

Pastor Mireille Desrosiers, thank you for establishing a prayer ministry that has greatly impacted my prayer life. I will never forget the many intercessory prayers that have been made on my behalf to see this vision become a reality.

Rev. Dr. Eversel Griffith, thank you for your contribution in helping me write my first book.

Dr. Anita Underwood, thank you for your contribution to this project. It is greatly appreciated.

Pastor Rebecca Simmons, my chief editor, thank you for your encouragement, patience, and guidance in helping me publish my first book.

Diligence Publishing Company and team, thank you for all the time and effort you have invested in publishing this book.

Lola Reid and NuVision Designs, thank you for creating an amazing cover design.

ORDER MY STEPS

Four Biblical Keys to Effective Decision Making

By Brenda J. Robinson

INTRODUCTION

Decision making is a skill many humans take a lifetime to perfect. If we had a crystal ball that could reveal the consequences of every decision we have made, we would find decision making extremely easy to do. Unfortunately, life does not work that way. The truth is, for every decision we make, there is a consequence to bear. If we make good choices in life with the help of God, we will experience some degree of happiness. If we make poor choices in life without His help, we can end up paying for them the rest of our lives.

Our decisions impact our present and our future. They also can have a resounding impact on those around us. Thus, it is crucial that we get them right. For example, when we choose our lifetime partner, we must be very sure we are making the right choice. If we wind up with the person that God did not approve for us, we could have a cross to endure. Choosing a soulmate not only affects you, but others, too. Many children today are psychologically damaged because of their parents' poor choices and lack of judgment.

The Bible presents us with a clear blueprint for making effective decisions. Solomon, the wisest man that ever lived, attained the secret to life in his later years. It is found in this simple, yet profound proverb:

Trust in the LORD with all thine heart; and lean not unto thine own understanding. In all thy ways acknowledge him, and he shall direct thy paths. (Proverbs 3:5, 6)

The wisdom in this one Bible verse is truly amazing! This proverb, known and quoted by many Christians, is often not implemented. Because we live in a society that teaches us to be self-sufficient and in control of our own destiny, many people struggle with trusting God with all their heart in their decision making. They find themselves, quite often, leaning to their own understanding. Trying to make sense about life and our circumstances can be overwhelming. However, we are instructed in the Bible to acknowledge God in all of our actions. By doing this, we will receive divine direction from God who gives peace and rest to the soul.

Solomon, one of the most accomplished kings in all of Israel's history, discovered this truth as one of the keys to living a happy and fulfilled life. After achieving all the power, wealth, honor, and knowledge that life could offer, he came to the conclusion that it is all meaningless without God at the forefront. He realized that a God-driven life is more valuable than a self-driven one. Having achieved much through his own selfish ambitions, he found that it did not bring him happiness. This is why he said "...And in all your getting, get understanding" (Proverbs 4:7 NKJV).

If we want to experience that real peace and abundant life that Jesus spoke about to His disciples, then we must let Him "Order Our Steps."

Peace I leave with you, my peace I give unto you: not as the world giveth, give I unto you. Let not

your heart be troubled, neither let it be afraid.
(John 14:27)

It is the only way to achieve ultimate satisfaction in your life. You may choose to walk life's path using your own logic and reasoning; however, as a human, you are imperfect and limited. If you choose your own course, you can end up on the wrong path and become disappointed, confused, or discouraged. You can also experience failure. Instead, let God direct your path. He is perfect, excellent, and prophetic. He never makes a mistake and He never fails. In addition, He can see farther into the future than you can. He is more than capable to lead your life onto paths you could never see or comprehend.

You do not need to spend your life making poor choices. Decide to be proactive and make right choices the first time around. Allow God, the Sovereign one, the Alpha and Omega, the Creator (Elohim) to guide your steps. He knows the pathway of life because He existed before the creation of time. He will lead you to a bright end.

As you commit your way to Him and trust also in Him, God will bring it to pass (Psalm 37:5). Are you looking for assistance to make the right decisions in your life? If so, God wants to help you. He understands life is filled with vicissitudes and uncertainties. In addition, He is fully aware of the crossroads, detours, and dead ends you may face along the journey. You can depend on Him to not lead you astray. Why not trust the One who not only KNOWS your future, but HOLDS it in His hands, especially during life's most challenging moments?

David wrote, "The steps of a good man are ordered by the LORD: and he delighteth in his way" (Psalm 37:23). Do you consider yourself a good person by God's standards? If so, take comfort in the fact that He already has a plan for your life. The Bible states, "For whom he foreknew, he also predestined to be conformed to the image of his Son" (Romans 8:29 WEB). In other words, because God has perfect knowledge, He has already preordained your steps in life towards something good and hopeful. He told the prophet Jeremiah, "For I know the plans I have for you, says the Lord. They are plans for good and not for evil, to give you a future and a hope" (Jeremiah 29:11 TLB). Yes, God is already ordering your steps if you have really committed your life to Him.

I recognized this truth during my teen years when I was seeking God for guidance in my life.

Because He was faithful in answering my prayers, I desired to follow His lead in my college and career choices, in my personal life and in my ministry. Although life has not been easy and I had my share of struggles and tears, I can honestly say that through it all, I have learned that God's way is the best way. What I have gained through my life experiences regarding this proverb, I have written to you in the pages to follow.

In this book, you will find four keys to effective decision making based on Proverbs 3, verses five and six. You will also find a life application section after each key presented. As you read through the book and closely examine its content, you will observe the wisdom in trusting an omniscient, all-powerful and immutable God. You will also ascertain why it is important to include Him in every detail of your life no matter how insignificant it may be. As you begin to ask God for guidance in every area and season of your life, you will discover Him to be faithful in "ordering your steps" onto fruitful and rewarding paths.

Trust God Wholeheartedly

"Trust in the L<small>ORD</small> with all your heart...."
(Proverbs 3:5 NKJV)

KEY ONE

Who can you trust? This is a question posed by many. With the rise of infidelity among married couples, deception among our national and spiritual leaders, sexual misconduct towards women, dangerous terrorists, and the list goes on, no wonder people are skeptical about trusting others. If you have ever been disappointed, misled, betrayed, abandoned, abused, cheated on, lied on, etc., by someone significant in your life such as a parent, a sibling, a spouse, a spiritual leader or a friend, you might have difficulties trusting someone again.

Although trusting others can be a struggle from time to time, it is necessary in order to function in life. Just as water is essential for physical living, trust is vital for daily and spiritual living. It is very hard to live in this world without trusting anyone. Every day we are forced to place our confidence in something or someone. For instance, we exercise faith in the schools to keep our children safe and to educate them. We expect our employers to pay us for our labor. We even rely on our banks to secure our money. Our world system requires us to trust one another. In order for us to have a relationship with Christ, we must learn to trust Him.

But without faith it is impossible to please him:
for he that cometh to God must believe that he is,
and that he is a rewarder of them that diligently
seek him. (Hebrews 11:6)

In Hebrews 11:6, we are told to trust God if we want to please Him and expect to receive anything from Him. It is hard to build a good, solid relationship with God without trust. From the beginning of time, God desired man to trust Him. When man was placed in the Garden of Eden, he was given his first test of trust. God gave him everything he could ask for: a perfect environment free from labor, worries and cares, the fat of the land, and dominion over everything. The only thing God asked man to do was trust Him enough NOT to eat from the tree of the knowledge of good and evil. WHY? Because, God knew the day man ate from the tree, he would be held accountable for this knowledge, and later, his actions. God also knew man would have to work hard in an environment—the earth—that would be cursed as a result of his disobedience. Moreover, man would be under the influence of the "prince of the power of the air," who steers everyone, unless he or she accepts Jesus Christ, on a path of destruction.

Enter through the narrow gate. For wide is the gate and broad is the road that leads to destruction, and many enter through it. (Matthew 7:13 NIV)

Because man wanted to satisfy his infatuation of being like God, he believed Satan's lie that he would become as wise as God if he ate from the tree. As a result of disobeying God's instructions, man lost his close relationship and sweet fellowship with a loving God. He is now left to live his life as he deems fit.

11

The good news is God is ready and willing to order our steps in life. He has an effective plan to bring us to our expected end. All we have to do is submit our will and way to Him and trust Him to do the rest.

Our Choice

We were created as free moral agents. Because God loved us so much, He gave us the choice to love and trust Him. God could have designed us as robots, heeding to His beck and call. However, He created us with our own minds so we could love and trust Him genuinely.

Have you ever seen people force others to love and trust them? It is a miserable thing. The person demanding love and trust is in denial because he or she is not receiving these things from the heart, and the one being forced to love and trust that person is unhappy because he or she is going through the motions without any real emotions. When you decide to trust God, you will be divinely favored.

O taste and see that the LORD is good: blessed is the man that trusteth in him. (Psalm 34:8)

When I look at people in the Bible that whole-heartedly placed their hope in God, their lives were greatly rewarded. Let us look at Job for a moment. Although Job was tested in measures I would not wish on my worst enemy, he was richly blessed at the end. He received double for his trouble.

He was tested in three major areas of life: family, finances, and health. God knows, just like He knew with Job, how much we trust Him in each of these areas in our lives. He knew Job loved Him dearly and trusted Him even in the darkest period of his life. He also knew how much Job could bear. God did not permit Job to endure any more than he could handle. As a result, Job was highly favored for his faith in God. Although he lost his children, health, finances and substances, he was restored twice as much as he had before (Job 42:10-16).

When you make the decision to trust in the Lord with all your heart, like Job, even if you do not understand what He is doing in your life, it will pay off. In essence, you are telling God that His credit is so good with you that you are willing to surrender your life and your situation to Him even in times of perplexity.

God yearns for His children to love and lean on Him in that manner. He bids us to come to Him as little children. We must have child-like faith when trusting God. You may notice that children believe every word their parents say. We must believe everything God says to us in His Word.

And said, Verily I say unto you, Except ye be converted, and become as little children, ye shall not enter into the kingdom of heaven. (Matthew 18:3)

Just as children depend solely upon their parents to meet their needs, we must whole-heartedly trust God to supply our needs. He has enough resources on Earth and in Heaven to provide for us regardless of the size of our need. He is the *El Shaddai*, a Hebrew word which means "God Almighty." He can supersede our expectations in any circumstance because He is the God of "more than enough." We just have to trust in His astounding ability to act on our behalf. The choice is ours. We can choose to trust in ourselves, the government or others to sustain us, or we can have faith in God who is well equipped to satisfy any lack in our lives.

God desires for us to trust Him like a father. The prophet Isaiah describes Christ as our everlasting Father (Isaiah 9:6). Our natural fathers are here today and gone tomorrow, due to death or other factors. Although they are called to be providers for their families, some fail to do so, even with the best intentions. God vows never to leave us nor forsake us (Hebrews 13:5). Everything in this world was created by Him and belongs to Him. Let us choose to place our complete confidence in God who stands by His Word and who has the power to bring to fruition whatever He promises.

So shall my word be that goeth forth out of my mouth: it shall not return unto me void, but it shall accomplish that which I please, and it shall prosper in the thing whereto I sent it.
(Isaiah 55:11)

God is Alpha and Omega

Allowing God to order our steps involves really knowing Him as Alpha and Omega.

I am Alpha and Omega, the beginning and the ending, saith the Lord, which is, and which was, and which is to come, the Almighty.
(Revelation 1:8)

When we recognize God as the Alpha and Omega, we believe that God existed before time and will exist after time. The words *Alpha* and *Omega* are Greek terms that mean *the beginning* and *the end*. Before the foundation of time, God predestinated us to be His children to fulfill His purpose in us.

Having predestinated us unto the adoption of children by Jesus Christ to himself, according to the good pleasure of his will. (Ephesians 1:5)

It is our responsibility as His sons and daughters to trust Him to achieve His good pleasure in us. He guarantees to perform it unto the appearing of Jesus Christ (Philippians 1:6). In other words, God will continue the process of making us whole and complete in Him until Jesus comes back for us. As the Alpha and Omega, He is well able to finish what He starts in us.

David, a man after God's own heart, went down the wrong path many times in his life. He committed adultery and murder and bore false witness against his neighbor. Yet, in spite of David's mistakes and shortcomings, God was not through with him. David knew he was a work in progress until God accomplished His purpose in his life.

It is not our job to finish what God starts in us. We do not have enough knowledge, talent or skill to do this apart from His Holy Spirit. Only God has unlimited power and inexhaustible resources to bring to maturity and correct those things in our lives that are undeveloped and need improvement.

For we are God's handiwork, created in Christ Jesus to do good works, which God prepared in advance for us to do. (Ephesians 2:10 NIV).

David understood this reality and uttered the following words: "The Lord will perfect that which concerns me; Your mercy, O Lord, endures forever; Do not forsake the works of Your hands" (Psalm 138:8 NKJV).

If we can accept the undeniable truth in the midst of our struggles that God is highly adept at producing GREATNESS IN US far above what we could ask or think, we would not feel so defeated about our weaknesses and struggles. As we surrender these things to God and release them into His hands, He can finish the work in us.

Now unto him that is able to do exceeding abundantly above all that we ask or think, according to the power that worketh in us.
(Ephesians 3:20)

The Alpha and Omega's work can only be accomplished through faith. If we continue to read His Word, we will grow in our faith.

So then faith comes by hearing, and hearing by the word of God. (Romans 10:17)

Can you trust Him today to complete whatever you have entrusted into His hands? It may be a personal matter, a family situation, a financial concern, an addiction, a medical condition, etc. Whatever it is, give it to Him today. He knows your beginning and end; and what will happen to you along life's journey. Trust him today to guide you in every step you make from start to finish.

Do not let Satan discourage you about the failures in your life, and especially the times when you failed even God. You can progress beyond your failures because He knew all of them before for you made them. God's plan your life encompasses your victories and failures. He has already made you to be triumphant in Christ Jesus. Walk in the victory God provides through Jesus Christ His Son!

Nay, in all these things we are more than conquerors through him that loved us.
(Romans 8:37)

God Loves and Cares for Us

Do you know that God loves us no matter what? It does not matter to Him who we are, where we have come from, what we look like or what we have done. God loves us regardless and unconditionally! His love for us is unlike any love we could ever feel or imagine.

Because God's love is "agape" in nature, He will NEVER stop loving us. *Agape* is a Greek term for love characterized by selfless, sacrificial, and unconditional acts. It is a love that best describes God's love for us. The Bible says, "But God commends his own love toward us, in that while we were yet sinners, Christ died for us" (Romans 5:8 WEB). In other words, God did not wait until we were worthy to be loved by Him; He displayed His love for us when we were in an unlovable state. Now, *that's* love!

We may be craving for someone to love us today. Or we may feel genuinely loved by a spouse, our family, or a friend. However, no one will love us or has the ability to love us unconditionally like God. *Agape* love originated from God and can only be experienced through God and through the working of the Holy Spirit in our hearts (Romans 5:5).

His infinite love for us is the reason why we can trust Him with our whole hearts and lives. He loves us too much to see us make poor decisions that will lead to discontentment or even destruction.

Some people find it difficult to forgive themselves for the bad choices they have made. However, the Bible teaches us that love will cover a multitude of sins (I Peter 4:8). God's love will cover anything we have done. His forgiveness has no boundaries or end. Thank God, He does not hold grudges or harbor ill feelings towards us when we do things that displease Him. God can simultaneously forgive us and forget the things we have done. The Bible states, "As far as the east is from the west, so far hath he removed our transgressions from us " (Psalm 103:12). In other words, our sin is erased from His memory the moment we ask Him to forgive us. Now that is mind boggling! However, the key to God's forgiveness is confession. When we are willing to admit our wrongdoings to Him, He will forgive us (1 John 1:9).

If a holy and righteous God can love and accept us with our flaws and blemishes, why can't we accept and love ourselves and better yet, others?

Focusing on God's amazing love and abundant forgiveness will help us in our struggle to be free from our guilt and shame. It will also help us to extend mercy to those who have hurt us and who need our forgiveness. Choose to receive God's incredible love for you!

Not only does God love us, but He truly cares for us and has our best interest at heart. No matter what state we find ourselves in, God is concerned about us and wants to help us. No matter how big or small the problem may be in our lives, God wants to handle it.

Give all your worries and cares to God, for he cares about you. (1 Peter 5:7 NLT)

The Bible states, "Since he did not spare even his own Son but gave him up for us all, won't he also give us everything else?" (Romans 8:32 NLT). We can count on God to accommodate us according to His riches in glory by Christ Jesus (Philippians 4:19). If we need physical strength, emotional stability, financial security, and so on, God will provide. If He can take the time to clothe the fowls of the air and the lilies in the field, how much more will He take the time to care for us?

"Therefore I say to you, do not worry about your life, what you will eat or what you will drink; nor about your body, what you will put on. Is not life more than food and the body more than clothing? Look at the birds of the air, for they neither sow nor reap nor gather into barns; yet your heavenly Father feeds them. Are you not of more value than they? Which of you by worrying can add one cubit to his stature?

"So why do you worry about clothing? Consider the lilies of the field, how they grow: they neither toil nor spin; and yet I say to you that even Solomon in all his glory was not arrayed like one

of these. Now if God so clothes the grass of the field, which today is, and tomorrow is thrown into the oven, will He not much more clothe you, O you of little faith?

"Therefore do not worry, saying, 'What shall we eat?' or 'What shall we drink?' or 'What shall we wear?' For after all these things the Gentiles seek. For your heavenly Father knows that you need all these things. But seek first the kingdom of God and His righteousness, and all these things shall be added to you. Therefore do not worry about tomorrow, for tomorrow will worry about its own things. Sufficient for the day is its own trouble." (Matthew 6:25-33 NKJV)

We are encouraged to seek God FIRST instead of worrying about how we will eat, drink, or get our other physical necessities met. He is fully aware of our needs even before we express them to Him. We are His highest creation. If He is concerned about all of the other creatures or creations on Earth, surely, He is concerned and cares about us. We need never to fret about His provision for us. Our responsibility is to simply trust Him and watch Him do what He does best— BE GOD.

When we are faced with a real crisis in our lives, whether it relates to our finances, our family, or our health, we can be assured that our Heavenly Father cares and is in the midst of our crisis. Not only can God meet our needs in a crisis situation, but He WILL meet our needs in a crisis situation. He loves us too much to see us go through a crisis alone.

The devil loves for us to get anxious about things we have no control over. We cannot control our fate when it comes to the physical matters of life. We do not have any say as to how the economy goes, or even our financial security. We can have a job today and lose it tomorrow due to downsizing. We can have investments today and lose them tomorrow due to a market crash. We can be married today and be given divorce papers tomorrow. We can be healthy one minute and the next minute be diagnosed with a terminal illness.

Therefore, let *Yahweh Jireh*, (the Hebrew word which means "The Lord Will Provide") handle those things in our lives. We are the apple of His eye (Psalm 17:8). He loves us and has given us everlasting consolation and good hope through His grace (2 Thessalonians 2:16). He is in control! He will not disappoint us! We will never lose when we make Him top priority in our lives and put our lives totally in His hands. He desires to be involved in our personal affairs to ensure our prosperity.

Blessed is the man who walks not in the counsel of the ungodly, nor stands in the path of sinners, Nor sits in the seat of the scornful; But his delight is in the law of the LORD, and in His law he meditates day and night. He shall be like a tree planted by the rivers of water, that brings forth its fruit in its season, whose leaf also shall not wither; and whatever he does shall prosper.
(Psalm 1:1-3 NKJV)

The children of Israel experienced His care when they wandered in the wilderness for 40 years. During those years, Israel was guided on their way by a "pillar of cloud" and a "pillar of fire." The pillars guided and protected Israel as they journeyed. Normally, the cloud by day and the fire by night moved in front of Israel to point the way. As Israel left Egypt, however, the cloud moved to the rear to provide protection from the Egyptians. The pillar of cloud guided them, and the pillar of fire demonstrated the presence of God.

So they took their journey from Succoth and camped in Etham at the edge of the wilderness. And the LORD went before them by day in a pillar of cloud to lead the way, and by night in a pillar of fire to give them light, so as to go by day and night. He did not take away the pillar of cloud by day or the pillar of fire by night from before the people. (Exodus 13:20-22 NKJV)

The Israelites knew that God was present with them even when they failed Him because they were His people. He also made provisions for them in the wilderness by providing manna from heaven.

Then the LORD said to Moses, "Behold, I will rain bread from heaven for you. And the people shall go out and gather a certain quota every day, that I may test them, whether they will walk in My law or not. And it shall be on the sixth day that they shall prepare what they bring in, and it shall be twice as much as they gather daily."
(Exodus 16:4, 5)

Although we may not always do everything to please God, He will still meet our needs like He did the children of Israel. He knew they were stiff-necked and disobedient to Him and His laws; nevertheless, He still showed them mercy and grace.

When we are absolutely convinced that God loves us and cares for us, it will not be so difficult for us to trust Him. We should continually remind ourselves, especially during discouraging times, how much God loves us and would move heaven and earth for us.

All Things Work Together for Good

One of my favorite scriptures in the Bible is Romans 8:28. It is a verse that everyone should keep in their memory bank.

And we know that all things work together for good to those who love God, to those who are the called according to His purpose.
(Romans 8:28 NKJV)

Life consists of good times and bad times, happy times and sad times. Everyone loves a pleasant season, free of tribulations and full of joy. Very few, if any, embrace an unpleasant season. However, all of the seasons of our lives have a purpose, and that purpose will work out for our good. The writer of the book of Hebrews tells us no difficult season is joyous at first, but it yields righteous results.

Now no chastening seems to be joyful for the present, but painful; nevertheless, afterward it yields the peaceable fruit of righteousness to those who have been trained by it.
(Hebrews 12:11 NKJV)

Many times, we desire God to develop the fruit of love, peace, joy, faith, goodness, kindness, gentleness, self-control and patience in our lives; however, we do not typically enjoy His method of producing these traits in us. Nevertheless, if we can stand the discipline it takes to yield the fruit of the Spirit in our lives, we will become fortified Christians.

Peter reassured the early church about the persecutions they were facing as followers of Christ. He wanted them to know their trials and afflictions were "blessings in disguise." They are designed to mature our faith and bring us honor at Christ's return.

That the trial of your faith, being much more precious than of gold that perisheth, though it be tried with fire, might be found unto praise and honour and glory at the appearing of Jesus Christ: (1 Peter 1:7)

Peter describes the shaking of our faith and confidence in God as a precious metal—gold. Gold is considered the most treasured metal on the planet. The more it is placed under heat, the more refined it becomes. Our faith is just like gold. The more it is tried in the fire of life, the more valuable it is to God and the stronger it becomes for us to believe God for any and everything; not just in this life but in the life to come!

When we ask God to guide us through each season of our lives, regardless of how favorable or unfavorable it may be, our lives will be enriched, and we will have a testimony to share with others.

But thanks be to God! For through what Christ has done, he has triumphed over us so that now wherever we go he uses us to tell others about the Lord and to spread the Gospel like a sweet perfume. (2 Corinthians 2:14 TLB)

It is part of the process He uses to "order your steps." Do not get side-tracked by the rough road you may have to travel along life's journey. If God is leading you to it, He will bring you through it. Will you allow Him to escort you through every path you take, convinced that it will lead to something good at the end? Why not rest in the One who promises to work everything out for the good of those who love Him?

Trusting God is not always an easy thing to do. It is a discipline that takes a great deal of time and patience. However, the more you practice it in your life, the more it becomes part of your life. Although it has not been easy for me to trust God in everything in my life, it is something God began to teach me early in my Christian walk. I can remember my first trust experience as a believer: when I learned to pray. At first, I did not know if I was praying right because I was not using many fancy words. I just talked to Him like I would talk to my mother or sister. I can remember saying to myself when I prayed, "I hope I am doing this right."

Even though I was not totally sure, I had to put my trust in God and believe that my prayers were being accepted and heard by Him. Guess what? The more I trusted in what I was doing, the more I became confident in my prayers. As a result, I developed a prayer life that connected me closer to God each time I prayed. As my relationship with Him became stronger, I began to trust God more. I also learned how to pray about major things in my life: my friends, my college, my family and my personal life.

I remember really trusting God when my family had to relocate from Newburgh to Spring Valley, New York. At first, I was excited about the relocation. The thought of meeting new friends and being in a new school environment really excited me. I was under the crazy notion that the grass would be greener on the other side...I was wrong. When I arrived at my new high school and saw how different it was from my former high school (a little smaller than my former junior high school), I panicked. I also became very homesick and wished I was back in Newburgh with my former friends, classmates, and teachers. I had to learn from that experience that God is the same everywhere. It does not matter where you travel in life; He will never leave you nor forsake you (Matthew 28:20).

It was through this situation that I realized God will be with you in the midst of any transition in your life regardless of its nature or your age. At that time, I was only sixteen. However, I still had to learn to trust in God who could help me make new friends and adjust to a new environment. I found out He is dependable. It was an experience I never forgot and that has carried me during other transitional periods in my life.

I also remember putting my trust in God to point me to the right college to attend. During my high school years, I prayed that God would place me at the college that was best for me. I knew there were many colleges to choose from, and I wanted to make sure I chose the one right for me. I ended up being accepted to and attending Pace University in New York. Although I was crushed when I was not accepted to the college of my choice, I discovered God knew best. I had a great experience at Pace that prepared me for my career. I also received the opportunity to work at IBM Corporation, which was located not too far from the school. After I graduated, I was offered an exempt position as an accountant with a good salary. I do not believe that opportunity would have been afforded to me had I not trusted God to "order my steps."

Today, I am determined to fight the good fight of faith, especially in the areas that I have been most challenged in trusting God. As I continue to live and grow in His grace and knowledge, I know that my trust in Him will only increase. I am glad I am learning to trust God even when He chooses a path for me different than the one I would have chosen.

Life Application

Key Verse:

God's way is perfect. All the LORD's promises prove true. He is a shield for all who look to him for protection. (Psalm 18:30 NLT)

Personal Reflection:

(1) Do I really *trust* God enough to *guide* my life?

(2) Am I convinced He knows what is *best for my life*?

(3) Do I undoubtedly believe *He loves me,* and genuinely *cares enough about me* to meet my needs?

(4) Do I have faith in His power to *work everything out for my good?*

Prayer Focus:

Lord, please help me to continually trust You, especially when I cannot see my way. You desire to order my steps and even more during difficult times. You have a proven track record of blessing those who trust You. This is why I want to put my complete confidence in You. Help me to constantly focus on Your love for me and be fully persuaded that You only want the best for me. I know You are working out every situation in my life for my good. Help me to trust You to finish the good work you started in me and perfect my personal challenges. In Jesus' name, Amen!

Do Not Rely on Your Own Intellect

"…And do not rely on your own insight or understanding." (Proverbs 3:5 AMP)

KEY TWO

Allowing God to "order our steps" requires us to not lean to our own understanding. For many of us, this is challenging. It is so easy to rely on our intellect when making decisions, especially if it makes perfect sense to us, or if it worked for us in the past. However, what worked for us in the past, may be ineffective for us today. Likewise, what was relevant in the past may be meaningless today. Although God has given all of us the ability to think and to reason, there will be times in our journey when we will have to make moves that go beyond our level of reasoning or understanding. In other words, we may have to take a leap of faith into the unknown and make a decision simply based upon what we feel God is placing on our *heart* to do, not necessarily what our *head* is telling us to do.

The Bible tells us that we walk by faith and not by sight (2 Corinthians 5:7). When we make decisions based ONLY on what we see or understand, we do not leave room for God to perform the unusual or supernatural in our lives. As a result, we could be missing out on a great opportunity for God's best for our lives. This is why we are encouraged to live a life of faith.

And those whose faith has made them good in God's sight must live by faith, trusting him in everything. Otherwise, if they shrink back, God will have no pleasure in them.
(Hebrews 10:38 TLB)

The Bible describes *faith* as "the substance of things hoped for and the evidence of things not seen" (Hebrews 11:1). It gives us examples of men and women who walked not according to their own knowledge or reasoning, but according to God and His Word, trusting and believing Him to direct their paths.

Abraham is a perfect example of a man with this kind of faith. He believed in God and exercised faith in our Heavenly Father. Unlike other people in his day who worshipped pagan gods, Abraham trusted in the one true God, the Supreme Being. Because of his faith in God, he was considered a "righteous man" (Romans 4:3).

One day he felt a strong charge from God to leave his country, his people, and his extended family, and travel to an unknown territory. It takes a great deal of faith and trust in God to leave everything behind and follow Him. Abraham had enough confidence in God to obey Him and was vastly compensated.

God had told Abram, "Leave your own country behind you, and your own people, and go to the land I will guide you to. If you do, I will cause you to become the father of a great nation; I will bless you and make your name famous, and you will be a blessing to many others. I will bless those who bless you and curse those who curse you; and the entire world will be blessed."
(Genesis 12: 1-3 TLB)

I am not going to tell you Abraham did not have some doubts; if so, I can understand.

41

Abraham could have considered God's request unreasonable, inconvenient or uncomfortable for him and his family. However, Abraham looked beyond these human feelings and trusted in the wisdom of God. He took a leap of faith, even when he did not know or even understand the outcome. He demonstrated a functional faith that worked in the midst of his circumstances. God wants us to exercise a faith that works despite the outcome.

Had Abraham let his pride get in the way of trusting and obeying God, he would have never been able to practice faith at this realm and would have missed God's abundant blessings for his life. Focusing too much on our feelings, our understanding, and our ability when God tells us to do something can lead to pride. Pride occurs when we refuse to adhere to God's instruction for our lives or receive His advice or help in our lives because of insecurity or overconfidence. Because pride is considered one of the seven things God hates (Proverbs 6:16-17), the Bible warns us against it. It will contribute to our downfall if we let it. God resists those who walk in pride but gives grace to those who walk in humility (James 4:6).

You may consider yourself a knowledgeable, reasonable and intelligent person. However, you may have to put all of that aside when you are trusting God. Leaning to your own understanding without considering God can lead you into trouble or create confusion in your life. If you can remember that God's thoughts are not our thoughts neither are His ways our ways (Isaiah 55:8), you will be ready to launch out on faith even when your path is not clear or is hard to grasp. The truth is your course of action does not always have to be logical to you. If God tells you to do something, just do it! Trust His directive and you will come out alright.

If Abraham had never stepped into the unknown and trusted God's foresight and insight, we probably would not be reading about the children of Israel today. Most of the Bible would not have been written and Jesus would not have descended through his lineage. It took one man's faith in God to put all of the above and more into motion. Praise God! What a lesson this is for us to trust in God with all our hearts and lean not to our own understanding.

God Knows Us Better than We Know Ourselves

Have you ever made a decision you lived to regret? A decision that looked and felt right to you at first, but later turned out to be a mistake? Sometimes, we let our emotions get the best of us and make decisions based on them. What we think and feel may not be the best choice for our lives. It is not uncommon for us to be wrong about someone or something. Most of us have had a change of heart regarding a decision we have made. We can avoid the anxiety of trying to make decisions based on our logic or feelings by letting God make them for us. Because He created us, He knows us better than we know ourselves.

O Lord, you have examined my heart and know everything about me. You know when I sit or stand. When far away you know my every thought. You chart the path ahead of me and tell me where to stop and rest. Every moment you know where I am. You know what I am going to say before I even say it. You both precede and follow me and place your hand of blessing on my head.

44

This is too glorious, too wonderful to believe! I can never be lost to your Spirit! I can never get away from my God! If I go up to heaven, you are there; if I go down to the place of the dead, you are there. If I ride the morning winds to the farthest oceans, even there your hand will guide me, your strength will support me. If I try to hide in the darkness, the night becomes light around me. For even darkness cannot hide from God; to you the night shines as bright as day. Darkness and light are both alike to you.

You made all the delicate, inner parts of my body and knit them together in my mother's womb. Thank you for making me so wonderfully complex! It is amazing to think about. Your workmanship is marvelous—and how well I know it. You were there while I was being formed in utter seclusion! You saw me before I was born and scheduled each day of my life before I began to breathe. Every day was recorded in your book!
(Psalm 139:1-16 TLB)

God knows what makes us upset and sad, and what makes us happy and cheerful. He is well acquainted with our temperament and our ways. I will admit I do not know what makes me happy all the time, although I may think I do. What contributes to my good mood today may cause me to be in a bad mood tomorrow. I am glad God knows my changes in moods and can relate to me accordingly. This is why I have chosen to let Him control my life. He knows how to put a smile on my face today, tomorrow, and in the subsequent years.

David is a good example of a man who understood this very thing. He knew God did a better job leading his life than he did. This is why he cried out to God on many occasions when he messed up. He was considered "a man after God's own heart" because of his willingness to please Him (Acts 13:22).

David was also conscious of his limitations. He did not have an issue with seeking God for help and forgiveness. Although David loved God with all of his heart and soul, he grieved God through his sin. God still had mercy upon him because David never failed to repent of his sins and ask God for help. God will have mercy on us if we repent of our sins and seek His support. In 1 John 1:9, it states, "If we confess our sins, He is faithful and just to forgive us our sins and to cleanse us from all unrighteousness."

Moreover, God had no problem forgiving David because of his contrite spirit. God never despises a person with a humble spirit and broken heart before Him (Psalm 34:18). Because David knew God as a loving and forgiving Father, he constantly looked to Him. He knew he could not trust himself. However, he could trust in the God of his salvation.

The Lord is my rock, and my fortress, and my deliverer; my God, my strength, in whom I will trust; my buckler, and the horn of my salvation, and my high tower. (Psalm 18:2)

David also saw God as his Shepherd. A shepherd is one who leads, guides, protects, and cares for his sheep. Sheep need a good shepherd because of their nature. These animals are known for their poor vision, foresight, and insight. They are also easily misled and prone to wander. David describes himself in Psalm 23 as a sheep with a good shepherd.

The Lord is my shepherd; I have all that I need. He lets me rest in green meadows; he leads me beside peaceful streams. He renews my strength. He guides me along right paths, bringing honor to his name. Even when I walk through the darkest valley, I will not be afraid, for you are close beside me. Your rod and your staff protect and comfort me. You prepare a feast for me in the presence of my enemies. You honor me by anointing my head with oil. My cup overflows with blessings. Surely your goodness and unfailing love will pursue me all the days of my life, and I will live in the house of the Lord forever. (Psalm 23 NLT)

Because God was his Shepherd, David did not need anything or have to want for anything. Do you want your needs and wants met?

David also described God as One who led him into peaceful situations. Do you want peace from your decision making?

David also found restoration in God. Life has a way of draining us physically, mentally, and spiritually. It can also deplete our physical and financial resources. It is good to know that God, our Shepherd, can restore the things life has taken from us, or things we have lost due to a bad decision.

Furthermore, David learned God will be with him in life threatening situations and at the end of life's journey. David was frequently running away from his chief enemy King Saul and his son, Absalom, who wanted him dead. We do not have to fear in times of distress or our enemies, because God is with us to comfort us. Even when death was upon him, David knew he did not have to be afraid because God was with him.

At the end of the Psalm, David expressed assurance that God would grant him goodness and mercy all the days of his life. Do you want goodness and mercy to follow you all the days of your life? Allow God to shepherd you. He knows the pathway to goodness and mercy.

Do Not Judge Your Life by Present Circumstances

Life is like a rollercoaster. You can be up today and down tomorrow. Things can be going well for you one minute: people speak well of you, marriage is great, money is good, body feels basically healthy, children are doing well, job is going well, church is booming, self-esteem is high, and life is good. Then, things began to turn south. For instance, tragedy hits, marriage goes bad, people tell "lies" about you, trouble arises in the home and on the job, bills start piling up (and not the ones you created), finances go under, sickness in your body and the list goes on. If you are not careful, you will feel defeated and lose hope in God. However, God is able to turn situations around for you and cause them to work in your favor.

I heard a preacher say, "It is what it is, but it is not what it seems." Life may be going really badly for us on the surface, but God may be working a miracle for us behind the scenes. If we judge our lives by our present circumstances, we will grow weary. Recognize that God has great intentions for our lives, and He is dedicated to carrying them through regardless of what may be happening in our lives.

When we look at the story of Joseph in the Bible (one of my favorites), we see God teaching us so much about not looking at our present circumstances. Joseph was a man who had a rough life from the moment God showed him a glimpse of his destiny. Do not think the devil is happy about the plans God has revealed to us about our future. He is plotting right now, like he did Joseph, for those plans not to come to pass. However, like Joseph, no demon in Hell can stop them from happening.

When Joseph's brothers tried to abort the dream by throwing him in the pit, God had a strategy already in motion to take him to the palace. Joseph had a rocky road to travel in route to his destiny, but it all worked out at the end for his good and for others. God had a master plan in place to lead him right to his position as Prince of Egypt. It did not look like it, judging his present circumstances, but it was in motion.

In his process to reach his next level in life, Joseph kept a positive attitude. Regardless of what circumstances he found himself in, and they were pretty horrible, Joseph constantly remained loyal to God. He knew God was with him all the time, and it was reflected in his attitude towards Him and others.

When Joseph was sold into slavery and ended up in Potiphar's house, he worked diligently and became the chief executor of Potiphar's affairs. Had Joseph become bitter due to the abandonment and rejection of his family, he would have never advanced to the next dimension in his life. Is your attitude holding you back from your next move?

Even when Joseph was thrown into prison for a crime he did not commit, he kept his integrity and faith in God. He also maintained a good attitude. As a result, Joseph was elevated to overseer of the prisoners, and then later the Prince of Egypt. As the Prince of Egypt, Joseph had the opportunity to take revenge against his brothers for the wrong they had done to him. However, Joseph took the high road and let his hurt from the past go. He forgave his brothers by blessing them in their time of famine.

Each step Joseph took prepared him for his next promotion in life and in God. Had Joseph held on to the hurt of his past from his brothers, he would have never experienced real progression in his life. Had Joseph not cooperated with the process, he certainly would not have been elevated to royalty.

God was taking Joseph through the *process of elevation*. We must go through a *process* in order to receive elevation in our lives, especially if we want to be promoted in God's Kingdom. Jesus, the author and finisher of our faith, went through a process while fulfilling His assignment on Earth, before receiving His position at the right hand of the throne of God.

Looking unto Jesus the author and finisher of our faith; who for the joy that was set before him endured the cross, despising the shame, and is

set down at the right hand of the throne of God.
(Hebrews 12:2)

God will be faithful in leading us, like He did Joseph, through the *process* to the *promise.* (Genesis 37, 39 - 41:1-44)

Are you cooperating with the process God is taking you through to get to your next position? When God is for you, He is more than anyone who tries to stand against you (Romans 8:31). No one has the power, including Satan, to stop you from flourishing or reaching the destiny God has designed for you. You can trust the process. Do not dwell on your present state or even your past hurts. Keep your focus on God. Know that He is working for you an eternal glory that far out-weighs your troubles.

For our light affliction, which is but for a moment,
worketh for us a far more exceeding and eternal
weight of glory (2 Corinthians 4:17).

Let God exceed your expectations today. He wants to order your steps through a process that may be far beyond what you can perceive or even fathom. Yes, it takes faith to believe in something you cannot see or comprehend. However, do not throw away your confidence in God. It has great value and yields exciting results!

So do not throw away your confidence; it will be richly rewarded. (Hebrews 10:35 NIV)

Remember the Unseen Realities

Making a decision based on the reality of our circumstances may not always be the right solution. I know we are often encouraged to "face reality" about situations that happen to us. We have heard the clichés, "wake up and smell the coffee" or "get your head out of the clouds and come down to earth." All of these statements imply that a person is living in denial and not facing some truth in his or her life.

Although life is filled with realities that cannot be ignored, we must also factor in the unseen realities of life that are paramount to consider in decision making. The Bible tells us to look beyond realities that we can see and trust in unseen realities—things which are not seen.

While we look not at the things which are seen,
but at the things which are not seen: for the
things which are seen are temporal; but the
things which are not seen are eternal.
(2 Corinthians 4:18)

An unseen reality we can never leave out of any decision in our lives is *God*. Even though we do not see God, we KNOW He exists. John lets us know that no man has seen God at any time (John 1:18). He is not visible to us with the naked eye. Even if we could see Him, we would not be able to look upon His face. Moses asked to see His glory, but God told him no man could see His face and live (Exodus 33:18-20).

God is an unseen reality that is always working for us. We can never take Him out of the equation of our circumstances. Even if our situation looks hopeless, dark and bleak, we know that with God all things are possible (Matthew 19:26). He is the mighty God who operates supernaturally *behind the scenes* in our lives.

When David was a shepherd boy, he placed his trust in an unseen reality fighting against the fully armored and terrifying Philistine giant, Goliath. Had David looked at the reality of his situation—his size and strength which were not a match for his opponent, Goliath—he would have never chosen to fight him. However, because David believed in an unseen reality, "God" who was a far mightier warrior than Goliath, he was able to face and defeat the giant (I Samuel 17:1-51).

The three Hebrew boys would have never stood against bowing to King Nebuchadnezzar and being thrown in a fiery furnace had they not believed in an unseen reality. The reality was these boys should have been consumed in the fire. However, an unseen reality, God, showed up in the fire with them and took the heat out of the flame. At the end, the three boys were delivered from the furnace and promoted by King Nebuchadnezzar (Daniel 3:1-30).

The *Word of God* is another unseen reality that operates powerfully *in* our lives and *for* our lives when we place our faith and hope in it. The Bible tells us the Word of God will stand forever:

The grass withereth, the flower fadeth: but the word of our God shall stand for ever.
(Isaiah 40:8)

It is the only thing we can absolutely trust. I am reminded of the story found in the book of Ezekiel. God showed the prophet Ezekiel a vision of a valley of dry bones. It represented Israel's devastation during their time of exile in Babylon. Many Israelites died during this time, and their city, Jerusalem, was left in ruins. The people were in a hopeless state and their hearts were fainting. Everything was dismal around Ezekiel.

God asked Ezekiel to prophesy over Israel's situation and say, "O dry bones, hear the word of the Lord!" (Ezekiel 37:4 NKJV). Although Ezekiel was faced with a disheartening situation, God asked him to believe in an unseen reality, His Word. When Ezekiel began to speak God's Word over Israel's circumstances, he began to see in the spirit realm, Israel's dead situation come to life (Ezekiel 36, 37:1-14).

When we speak the Word of God over dead situations in our lives, we can bring life to them. Releasing God's Word in the atmosphere enables God to breathe life on our situations. It not only changes our circumstances, but also changes us. It quickens our spirits and increases our faith. The Word of God is an unseen reality that must be considered when making any decision for our lives. It is not about what we see in the natural realm regarding our present state, it is about what we do not see—the Word of God, and what IT says about our situation.

Learn to pray the scriptures over your life and your circumstances. Practice this activity consistently in your life. You will be astonished by its powerful results! The *Word of God* is an unseen reality that produces much fruit in our lives when planted in the right soil of our hearts, souls and spirits, and watered by faith.

When God Does Not Make Sense

Has God ever directed you to do something that made absolutely no sense to you? I am sure all the things Joseph went through after God revealed to him a snapshot of his fate made little sense to him. When it seemed as if Joseph was taking two steps forward towards his destiny, he ended up taking three steps backwards. Shortly after being promoted to chief executor of Potiphar's affairs, Joseph ended up as a prisoner in jail for not compromising his integrity and allegedly committing adultery with Potiphar's wife (Genesis 39:1-20).

There will be times when we will wonder what God is doing *for* us, *through* us, *with* us, *to* us and *in* us. He does not always disclose these things to us. He certainly does not reveal to us all of His plans for us. He wants us to trust Him even when we cannot trace Him.

When we turn our faith loose and trust God, we release Him to touch our lives. If we doubt Him, even during times of uncertainty, we will literally tie His hands from performing His best in our lives. The only thing that prevents God from performing His best in our lives is our lack of faith. Jesus actually could not do miracles in one town during His earthly ministry because of the people's disbelief.

Coming into his own country, he taught them in their synagogue, so that they were astonished, and said, "Where did this man get this wisdom, and these mighty works? Isn't this the carpenter's son? Isn't his mother called Mary, and his brothers, James, Joses, Simon, and Judas? Aren't all of his sisters with us? Where then did this man get all of these things?" They were offended by him. But Jesus said to them, "A prophet is not without honor, except in his own country, and in his own house." He didn't do many mighty works there because of their unbelief. (Matthew 13:54-58 WEB)

It did not make sense to the people in town that Jesus, the carpenter's son, would speak with such wisdom and do such mighty works. God could not possibly be using Him? They knew Him "when." Do we doubt God when He uses something or someone we do not expect to bless us?

When God used the prophet Elisha to bless Naaman, His method to heal him did not make any sense. Although Naaman was the Commander in Chief of the King of Syria's army and a great hero, he was a leper. He needed a healing that only God could do. When Naaman went to the prophet to receive his healing, he was told to dip in the Jordan River seven times. Because this river was dirty and muddy, Elisha's instructions were absolutely ludicrous to Naaman. At first, Naaman refused to follow Elisha's directions. After being encouraged by his officers to give it a try, Naaman dipped himself seven times in the river and his body became as healthy as a little child's. If Naaman had relied on his own intellect and not followed the prophet's word, he would have never been healed of leprosy (2 King 5:1-14).

I am also reminded of the story of Abraham when God told him to sacrifice Isaac. He and Sarah were promised a son when he was seventy-five and she was sixty-five. Because Sarah was well past childbearing years, she laughed when God told Abraham they would have a child in their old age. For twenty-five years, they waited for Isaac, the promised child (Genesis 17:15-19; Genesis 18:1-15).

In the interim, Abraham and Sarah did something God never wants us to do. They decided to help God out and produce a seed through Sarah's handmaid, Hagar. Abraham and Sarah paid a terrible price for it through the birth of Ishmael (Genesis 16:1-16). We are still reaping the repercussions of that decision today—feud between the Jews and Arabs over the Promised Land.

Years later, God asked Abraham to offer up Isaac as a sacrificial offering to Him. Why would God ask Abraham to give up a son He promised him? Although it did not seem like God would make such a request, He did, and Abraham obeyed. Just when Abraham was about to give up his beloved son, Isaac, God furnished a ram in the bush for him to sacrifice (Genesis 21:1-5, 22:1-13).

Like Abraham, sometimes God will test our faith in order for us to see if we will really trust Him enough to surrender our best to Him. We will never lose out when we give God our very best.

My niece Janelle has tremendous faith; since she spends time with God in prayer, she has developed an ear to hear His voice clearly. God told her one day to sell her van. My mother gave her that van so she could travel back and forth to school from Rockland to Westchester; it was her only vehicle of transportation. When Janelle told me she kept hearing God say to sell the van, I doubted her since it did not make sense to me that God would tell her to sell something that was her only means of transportation. I asked Janelle how she was going to get back and forth to school without a car. I knew Janelle, being a student and all, did not have a job that paid enough money that would enable her to get another vehicle. She told me she did not know and that all she knew was that God was telling her to sell the van now. Janelle went to a Toyota dealer because that is where God showed her to go. They worked out a deal with her whereby they gave her top dollar for her van in exchange for a beautiful used Camry with low, affordable monthly car payments.

Had Janelle trusted in her own perception, she would have never sold the van. First, she did not have a lot of monthly income. How could she afford to make a car payment with little income? On top of that the amount she desired to pay was very minimal. Secondly, most car dealers will not give you a loan without a permanent job. What made her think they would give her a loan with a temp job? What man says is impossible, God says is possible:

Jesus said to him, "If you can believe, all things are possible to him who believes."
(Mark 9:23 NKJV)

Although Janelle's scenario did not make sense in the natural realm, it made sense in the spiritual realm. Had Janelle not obeyed God and sold the van at that time, she would have missed out on that particular car. It was definitely a blessing with her name on it! When we rely solely on our intellect, we will miss out on God's best for our lives. It absolutely pays to obey God even when it looks as though the path is not the wisest one.

There are endless possibilities and opportunities for us when we place our trust in God. There is so much we have yet to discover about God. God wants to reveal Himself to us in ways we have never seen before. If we try to figure Him out or think we have Him figured out in our lives, we will come up short or He will surprise us. Our job is to simply trust in His infinite wisdom and let Him *order our steps*. He will steer us in the right direction like He steered my niece Janelle.

In 1994, I felt God directing me to make a career change from the business world to the education sector. It was not until 1996, that I enrolled in a graduate program to fulfill my desire to become a school counselor. Although I always loved education, I decided during my under-graduate studies to pursue a career in business. At that time, I felt the business industry would offer me more opportunities and room for advancement than the education field. Later, I discovered that "helping people" was my passion, and therefore I decided to pursue it.

Before completing my degree, I had to complete two school internships. I chose my former high school as the place to complete one of my educational internships. After meeting with the assistant principal of the school, I was offered the internship. I was very excited about giving back to my alma mater, my community and my people. My internship experience was wonderful— one I will never forget! I enjoyed working with the students, faculty and staff.

Upon the completion of my internship, I applied for a job in the school district. It was the perfect scenario. I lived only three minutes walking distance from the school. It was also a great opportunity for me to make a difference in my community. However, I was not offered the position. I was crushed and highly disappointed. It was hard for me to accept the fact this school district was NOT God's perfect choice for my life.

However, I ended up working for a school district that I absolutely love. It is my current placement. I am happy and proud to be there. Had God given me the school district of my choice, the one I thought was right for my life, I would have been miserable. A few years later, the same school district had many challenges such as teacher layoffs and delays in signing teacher contracts.

Even though I was happy that God had ordered my steps to this school district, it was not "a walk in the park." At first, my new career as a school counselor was challenging. I started out with a part-time counseling position that barely paid the bills. To make ends meet, I took on three part-time jobs. Although I struggled financially in my new career, I strongly believed I was fulfilling God's desire for my life. Even in times of discouragement, I had to constantly pray for strength and stay focused on fulfilling my dream of being a full-time school counselor. I was determined to persevere and trust God even when my journey was rough. I knew I could not rely on my own intellect or feel defeated because of my financial situation. I had to trust God's wisdom and knowledge in deciding what was best for my life.

A few years later, I was offered a full-time position in the district. The struggle was finally over, and better times were ahead of me. What a blessing this decision for my life has been! I am glad God ordered my steps in choosing the right career and employer.

Life Application

Key Verse:

"For My thoughts are not your thoughts, Nor are your ways My ways," says the Lord.
(Isaiah 55:8 NKJV)

Personal Reflection:

(1) Do I trust God when He leads me to an *unfamiliar path*?

(2) Am I *cooperating* with the *process* God uses to fulfill His plan for my life?

(3) Do I trust in *unseen realities*?

(4) Am I obedient to God even when *He does not make sense* to me?

Prayer Focus:

Lord, order my steps in fulfilling Your plan for my life. Help me not to rely solely on my intellect when making life decisions but to seek Your Holy Spirit for guidance. You know what makes me happy. Please have Your way in my life even when it does not make sense to me. Help me not to judge my life by my present situation and make decisions accordingly. Let me focus on *unseen realities* I cannot see in the natural realm. You are working behind the scenes to bring me out victoriously, beyond my imagination. Thank you! In Jesus' name, Amen!

Pray About Everything

"Seek His will in all you do..." (Proverbs 3:6 NLT)

KEY THREE

God desires to be a part of every detail of our lives. In order for us to include Him in everything we do, we must *pray. Prayer* is essential for every believer. It connects us to God. Through prayer, we can communicate our deepest thoughts and feelings to God.

The Bible encourages us to pray: "With all prayer and petition pray [with specific requests] at all times [on every occasion and in every season] in the Spirit, and with this in view, stay alert with all perseverance and petition [interceding in prayer] for all God's people"

(Ephesians 6:18 AMP). In other words, always *pray about everything*—for every situation and for everyone! PRAY FOR YOUR FAMILY. PRAY FOR YOUR MARRIAGE. PRAY FOR YOUR CHILDREN. PRAY FOR YOUR COMMUNITY. PRAY FOR YOUR CHURCH. PRAY FOR YOUR COUNTRY. PRAY FOR THE PRESIDENT. PRAY FOR THE NATIONS.

The list can go on about the things and people we need to pray for. This especially holds true in decision making. *Praying about everything* should be our daily activity. Because we are consumed each day with choices, we should be constantly asking God to "help us."

I love to sing and reflect on the old hymn, "What a Friend We Have in Jesus." This song reminds me of the kind of friend Jesus wants to be to each of us. When we learn to take everything to Him in prayer, we will find Him to be the best friend ever!

As you read the words of the hymn, consider your friendship with Jesus. Have you allowed Him to be that kind of friend in your life?

What a friend we have in Jesus,
All our sins and griefs to bear!
What a privilege to carry
Everything to God in prayer!

O what peace we often forfeit,
O what needless pain we bear,
All because we do not carry
Everything to God in prayer.

Have we trials and temptations?
Is there trouble anywhere?
We should never be discouraged;
Take it to the Lord in prayer.
Can we find a friend so faithful
Who will all our sorrows share?
Jesus knows our every weakness;
Take it to the Lord in prayer.

Are we weak and heavy-laden,
Cumbered with a load of care?
Precious Savior, still our refuge—
Take it to the Lord in prayer.
Do thy friends despise, forsake thee?
Take it to the Lord in prayer!
In His arms He'll take and shield thee,
Thou wilt find a solace there.

Prayer helps strengthen our friendship with
God. If we want to have a better relationship and
friendship with God, we must communicate with
Him on a daily basis. Throughout our day, we

should be talking to God, asking for His advice, thanking and praising Him for everything He is doing and providing for us for the day. Acknowledging Him throughout the day will make our day run smoothly and be more productive. He desires to hear from us.

The Bible tells us "men ought to always pray and not faint" (Luke 18:1). The more we pray, the less anxious we will feel about things. God is ready, willing and able to grant the petitions of our hearts. All we have to do is make our requests known to Him.

In nothing be anxious, but in everything, by prayer and petition with thanksgiving, let your requests be made known to God. And the peace of God, which surpasses all understanding, will guard your hearts and your thoughts in Christ Jesus. (Philippians 4:6-7 WEB)

In the scriptures, we find Jesus constantly looking to His Father for guidance. He prayed about everything when He lived on Earth. Because Jesus knew the importance and power of prayer, He would often ascend to the mountainside and pray. Sometimes He prayed all night in order to gain the strength and direction

He needed in fulfilling His earthly calling (Luke 6:12).

When faced with the toughest decision of His life: to die on the cross for the sins of mankind, He prayed to His Father. He knew He was the chosen lamb needed to be sacrificed. However, wrapped in human flesh, Jesus did not find His assignment easy. In intense agony, Jesus prayed to His Father, as sweat fell from His face like drops of blood falling to the ground, earnestly pleading for strength to endure the crucifixion before Him (Luke 22:44).

In John 17, we find Jesus not only praying for Himself, but also for His current and future followers. He knew that only God could keep them and protect them from Satan and his evil doings. Because greater satanic forces would rise in the future against His followers in carrying out the mission of the church in the earth, Jesus prayed for them to have a greater anointing to withstand the evil days ahead. He also petitioned His Father to make them holy and teach them His Word. We know we cannot be pure or live holy on our own. It takes the work of the Holy Spirit moving in our hearts and purifying us constantly through the Word of God so we can walk blamelessly before Him.

Moreover, Jesus prayed for unity amongst all believers as He and His father were unified. Jesus knew that unity was the key to His believers' effectiveness and productivity in the world. There was nothing Jesus could not accomplish on earth without being united with His father. We know that unity is important because where there is unity there is strength.

If Jesus, being human and divine, felt the need to consult His Heavenly Father about everything, how much more should we seek God about everything? He is our chief example on how vital it is to have a consistent prayer life.

The hymn writer put it so aptly, "O, what peace we often forfeit, O, what needless pain we bear, all because we do not carry EVERYTHING to GOD in prayer." Let this be our daily request: "Lord, order my steps."

Acknowledge Him Through Worship

We should always begin our prayers with *worship*. *Worship* is the heartfelt act of glorifying, praising and exalting God. God LOVES worship. He is constantly looking for it. Man, God's highest creature, was created to worship Him. We are never out of order when we worship and praise God. The Bible indicates that praise actually looks good on us.

Rejoice in the LORD, you righteous ones; Praise is becoming and appropriate for those who are upright [in heart—those with moral integrity and godly character]. (Psalm 33:1 AMP)

Worship is not only appropriate for believers, but it is also good for us. It helps us concentrate on the One who has all power, wisdom and knowledge in assisting us to make the best choices for our lives. Decision making can be very stressful, especially when we feel pressured to find a solution. When we begin our day with worship and stay focused on Him, any decision we have to make throughout the day will not seem so stressful or complicated. God is constantly looking for opportunities to get our attention so He can "lighten our load" in making decisions. He wants to be the center of our universe and joy. This can only happen as we grow in worship. We honor Him when we include Him in our plans.

Worship also keeps us hopeful regarding our present and future circumstances. When we center our minds on our Heavenly Father; and how loving, merciful, faithful, good, forgiving, and caring He is, our spirits are lifted and our hope is kept alive.

God wants to function in full strength in our lives. Worship permits Him to do so. When we engage in worship, we touch His heart; and He is moved to perform miracles for us.

Do you need a miracle today? My definition of a miracle is a divine intervention of something that is beyond nature or human control. I am sure you can think of many things in your personal life, your family, your church, your neighborhood, your country and so forth that need divine intervention.

Begin to increase your worship to God so you can release His supernatural power in your personal and family matters. There is a peace that will flood your soul when you know God is in control of the affairs of your life and working remarkably for you.

It is important to note that the devil does not like us actively and consistently involved in worship. He does not want us focusing on God's character or recognizing Him as the King of kings and Lord of lords. He definitely does not want us to know God as *Elohim*, the Strong One or as *El*

Gibor, the Mighty Warrior. He is afraid of the confidence we gain by being in God's presence and worshipping Him. As we concentrate on the attributes of God, we diminish the devil's power over us by becoming empowered in our minds that we serve an all-powerful God.

On the other hand, God is constantly calling us to worship Him. Not only through the physical activity of raising our hands and lifting our voices in His presence, but also through our lifestyles. Being devoted to God and dedicated to Christian service are our "reasonable services." Our Heavenly Father should not have to compete for our affection. Nothing should be more precious to us than God. No one should be worthier of our commendation than God.

In Exodus 20:1-7, we find God commanding supreme loyalty from His chosen people—the Israelites.

And God spake all these words, saying,

I am the LORD thy God, which have brought thee out of the land of Egypt, out of the house of bondage.

Thou shalt have no other gods before me.

Thou shalt not make unto thee any graven image, or any likeness of any thing that is in heaven above, or that is in the earth beneath, or that is in the water under the earth.

*Thou shalt not bow down thyself to them, nor serve them: for I the L*ORD *thy God am a jealous God, visiting the iniquity of the fathers upon the children unto the third and fourth generation of them that hate me;*

And shewing mercy unto thousands of them that love me, and keep my commandments.

*Thou shalt not take the name of the L*ORD *thy God in vain; for the L*ORD *will not hold him guiltless that taketh his name in vain.*

As depicted in these verses, God will not share His glory with anyone. There was a generational blessing declared over Israel when they worshipped Him only and a generational curse when they rejected Him.

Worship is also displayed through our giving. When we give God our absolute best—our time, talent and resources, we are saying to Him with our actions, "God, You mean more to me than anything. Because You are Wonderful, I want to give You everything and acknowledge You in everything."

When we humble ourselves, and give HIM OUR BEST, He will give us HIS BEST in return.

Start acknowledging God in your life through worship. Mediate and worship Him as *El Ro'i*, the God of Seeing—One who lives and sees all that we do and endures. Celebrate Him as *Jehovah Jireh*, the God who provides—One who will provide anything you need during any season of your life. He is *Jehovah Shalom*, the God of our Peace—One who will maintain peace in all areas and seasons of your life.

The Prophet Isaiah described Jesus as Wonderful, Counselor, the Mighty God, Everlasting Father and the Prince of Peace (Isaiah 9:6). Do you find Him to be wonderful in your life? Let Him make wonderful decisions for you. He is the greatest counselor you will ever know. His advice is "out of this world." You will not find anyone on the planet mightier than Him. You can always count on Him to be a Father who makes excellent provisions for His children and loves them eternally.

Lastly, you will not experience true peace until you let Jesus, the Prince of Peace, rule your mind, body, soul and spirit.

Pray for His Will

⌒

When we acknowledge God through prayer, we should always pray in *His perfect or divine will*. This is His utmost desire for us in prayer. Jesus taught the disciples to pray, "Your kingdom come, your will be done on earth as it is in heaven" (Matthew 6:10 NKJV). God desires to reign in the hearts of men and women as He reigns in heaven. We have a choice to let Him rule our lives or run our own lives. Because He is a wise and sovereign God, it is only befitting for us to let Him rule.

He knows the road which leads to a satisfying life. There is righteousness, peace and joy in the Holy Ghost when we allow Him to reign as King over our lives. The Kingdom of God guarantees it!

For the kingdom of God is not meat and drink; but righteousness, and peace, and joy in the Holy Ghost. (Romans 14:17)

We may not fully appreciate or apprehend His plan for us, but it is the securest way to live. The scripture tells us, "Commit thy way unto the Lord; trust also in him; and he shall bring it to pass"

(Psalm 37:5). When we learn to turn everything over to Him in prayer, and trust Him, we will see Him do great exploits for us.

Allowing God to perform His will in our lives covers us under His divine protection. Evil cannot overtake us. Our enemies will not triumph over us. No weapon formed against us shall prosper (Isaiah 54:17). We are also assured of God's favor to help us during our time of need (Hebrews 4:16).

Let me be clear: Life is not perfect when you are in His perfect will. We live in an imperfect world with imperfect people. However, your life will be productive, and your joy will be fulfilled when you live life and do things God's way.

Some people have difficulties praying in God's will because of fear. They fear being unhappy if they do not get what they prayed for, or if they let God do the choosing. In Psalms 37:4 it states, "Delight yourself in the Lord, and He will give you the desires and petitions of your heart" (AMP). In other words, when we take pleasure in God and His will for us, He will grant us the desires and petitions of our hearts. We must remember that He knows how to please us better than we know how to please ourselves. If we really know the love of God, and we are really convinced He loves us, then His love cancels out all fear in our lives.

There is no fear in love; but perfect love casts out fear, because fear involves torment. But he who fears has not been made perfect in love.
(1 John 4:18 NKJV)

God loves us more than our hearts and minds can conceive. It is the trick of the enemy to make us feel God does not know how to satisfy us and that God does not love us. That is a lie from the pit of Hell! Our Heavenly Father knows how to make us glad. He gave us His very best, Jesus, so that through Him we would receive all that we need to be spiritually whole.

How we praise God, the Father of our Lord Jesus Christ, who has blessed us with every blessing in heaven because we belong to Christ.
(Ephesians 1:3 TLB)

Just like earthly parents can satisfy their children, God does too, but more. He has excellent knowledge and insight into our thoughts and feelings. Satan is the one who feeds our minds with lies about love and happiness. He does not know us like God KNOWS us, nor does he love us like God LOVES us. Satan's love is conditional. God's love has NO STRINGS ATTACHED!!!

I strongly believe the divorce rate in the church and outside the church is high because couples failed to pray in the will of God before they said "I do." I know your relationship with that man or woman may seem right today. However, God knows what lies ahead for you as a couple. He knows if your love will stand the test of time. Why not ask God to order your steps when it comes to marrying the right person and getting married at the right time? He knows what two hearts belong together, and when they are ready for each other.

Asking God to bless a decision we have made without consulting Him first is not praying in the will of God. Because God gave us free will, He will not force His will on us. Even though it is God's intention for all men to be saved and live according to His Word, the choice is ours to make. He has given us the Bible as a guide to find Him, live for Him and please Him. It is our roadmap to success and eternal life. If we fail to follow it, it is our loss.

When we do not seek His will for our lives, but pursue our own will, we end up in His permissive will. God will permit our desires and aspirations in life to happen, even if He knows it is not the best for us; or what He had in mind for us. When we fall in the permissive will of God, we fail to experience God's best for our lives. Although His grace is always sufficient for His children, whether they are in His divine will or permissive will, it is at a greater level when we are in His divine will. Although we are not exempt from struggles living in His perfect will, we have greater struggles when we are living in His permissive will.

When we do not pray for God's discretion about a thing or if we do not acknowledge Him in our decision making, we are, in essence, asking Him to permit what we desire. For example, we should not pray, "Please God, help me to attain this job," unless we start or end the prayer with "if it be your will." Why? Because, the job may not be as glamorous as it appears to be. We may actually grow to despise it in the long run or lose it sooner than expected.

On the other hand, we should pray, "Lord, is this job right for me?" Or "God, do You want me to have this position?" Or "God, place me in Your will so I will be happy in the long run." Why? Because He knows how to satisfy our longing hearts and give us good success.

Israel struggled following God's purpose for them as a nation. Because they were His chosen people, they were not supposed to mingle with other nations, nor eat the same food other nations ate. They were required to worship the God of Abraham. Other nations, however, worshipped pagan gods rather than the true living God. It was God's design that through Israel all the other nations would be blessed and the Messiah would come. His entire purpose to restore and redeem mankind from sin began with Israel. Because they did not want to be different from other nations, the Israelites had a difficult time adhering to God's laws and statues for them. Because of poor choices, they often fell into idol worship and sinned against God. As a result, God sent His judgment upon them through captivity: they were captured by nations stronger and more wicked than they were.

Although the Israelites made decisions out of the will of God, they were given chances to repent and be restored back to God. God used prophets such as Isaiah, Elijah, Elisha, Jeremiah and others to warn Israel: to repent and turn back to Him; of His coming judgment; and of His future plan of restoration.

Like Israel, we make choices contrary to God's will. However, God never stops loving us, nor gives up on us. He steadily looks for opportunities to help us make things right. All we have to do is express godly sorrow and turn back to Him.

In Samuel 8:4-22, we find Israel desiring a king like other nations. God told the prophet Samuel He wanted to be Israel's king. However, the nation begged Samuel to give them a king, overriding God's option for them. God was not being difficult when He did not want them to have a king. He knew it was not time for them to be ruled by a king. He had a king destined to rule the nation in the future. However, the people could not wait, and chose Saul.

In the beginning, Saul was a successful king. He consulted God about everything and obeyed His instructions. However, he got lifted in pride by derailing from God's plan, thus ruling the nation according to his terms. As a result, he and the nation suffered.

During Saul's reign, God revealed to Samuel that David was His choice as Israel's future king. Samuel was perplexed by God's selection for them because of David's outward appearance. At the time, David was a little shepherd boy, the youngest of Jesse's sons. God had to remind the prophet Samuel that man looks on the outward appearance, but He looks at the heart (I Samuel

16:7). Although David did not look like a king, he had a heart for God, and that is what God wanted.

Are you rejecting God's will for your life because it does not look or feel right to you? Do not make the mistake of judging something on the outside or someone on the surface. God knows the heart of the matter and the heart of the person. Let Him guide your heart so you can be content.

Pray for Wisdom and Understanding

I know you have heard the saying "The older you get, the wiser you become." Although this is a very true statement, I am discovering that wisdom does not have to be acquired only in your latter years or through your life's experiences. The Bible encourages us to pray for wisdom if we do not have it. Most young people are not mature in wisdom, so it is a perfect time in their lives to ask for it.

If any of you lacks wisdom, you should ask God, who gives generously to all without finding fault, and it will be given to you. (James 1:5 NIV)

I am reminded in the book of I Kings, Chapter 3, when God told Solomon to ask whatever he wanted from Him. Solomon was a young man when He ruled the nation of Israel. Because Solomon desired to rule Israel well, he asked God for an understanding heart to judge the people. God was so impressed with Solomon's request that He promised to make him the wisest man that ever lived.

Now the king went to Gibeon to sacrifice there, for that was the great high place: Solomon offered a thousand burnt offerings on that altar. At Gibeon the Lord appeared to Solomon in a dream by night; and God said, "Ask! What shall I give you?" And Solomon said: "You have shown great mercy to Your servant David my father, because he walked before You in truth, in righteousness, and in uprightness of heart with You; You have continued this great kindness for him, and You have given him a son to sit on his throne, as it is this day. Now, O Lord my God, You have made Your servant king instead of my father David, but I am a little child; I do not know how to go out or come in. And Your servant is in the midst of Your people whom You have chosen, a great people, too numerous to be numbered or counted. Therefore, give to Your servant an understanding heart to judge Your people, that I may discern between good and evil. For who is able to judge this great people of Yours?" The speech pleased the Lord, that Solomon had asked this thing. *Then God said to him: "Because you have asked this thing, and have not asked long life for yourself, nor have asked riches for yourself, nor have asked the life of your enemies, but have asked for yourself understanding to discern justice, behold, I have done according to your words; see, I have given you a wise and understanding heart, so that there has not been anyone like you before you, nor shall any like you arise after you. And I have also given you what you have not asked: both riches and honor, so that there shall not be anyone like you among the kings all your days. So, if you walk in My ways, to keep My statutes and My commandments, as your father David walked, then I will lengthen your days." (I Kings 3: 4-14 NKJV)*

The Greek terms for *wisdom* and *understanding* are "*Sophia*" and "*Phronesis*," respectively. *Sophia* means to have keen insight into the true nature of things. *Phronesis* refers to good judgment, or the skill to govern our life in a careful, successful manner. When you study the Greek meaning of these two words, it is clear that God is the source of wisdom and understanding. Only God can help us discern matters of the heart. God will also feed us with the intuition needed in figuring out the best decisions that will lead to the best results for our lives.

The book of Proverbs is filled with nuggets of wisdom. Solomon emphasizes in his writings the value of wisdom, instruction, wise counsel and understanding during one's earlier years:

The proverbs of Solomon the son of David, king of Israel; To know wisdom and instruction; to perceive the words of understanding; To receive the instruction of wisdom, justice, and judgment, and equity; To give subtilty to the simple, to the young man knowledge and discretion. A wise man will hear, and will increase learning; and a man of understanding shall attain unto wise counsels: To understand a proverb, and the interpretation; the words of the wise, and their dark sayings. The fear of the LORD is the beginning of knowledge: but fools despise wisdom and instruction. My son, hear the instruction of thy father, and forsake not the law of thy mother: For they shall be an ornament of

grace unto thy head, and chains about thy neck.
(Proverbs 1:1-9)

These verses contain sound advice for anyone, especially young people. Solomon was instructing his son when he was a young man to seek for wisdom. You are never too young to obtain wisdom and get understanding. Some of your most critical decisions in life will be made in your early adult years. When you learn to make wise choices in those years, you will avoid some heartaches in your latter years.

Solomon also advises his son to fear God; for it is the beginning of wisdom (Proverbs 1:7). As we develop a reverential fear for God, we will increase in godly wisdom.

Many people wish they could turn back the clock and make better choices. You heard the saying, "If I knew then, what I know now, life would be different." In other words, if I had only applied wisdom in my younger years, my latter years would be different.

The good news is, it is never too late to find wisdom and gain understanding. All we have to do is go to the source—God. He is willing to give us these two virtues. The more we pray for wisdom and understanding, the more we will obtain them from God.

Take time to pray for wisdom and understanding. David prayed on several occasions for understanding.

Give me understanding, and I shall keep thy law; yea, I shall observe it with my whole heart. (Psalm 119:34)

Thy hands have made me and fashioned me: give me understanding, that I may learn thy commandments. (Psalm 119:73)

I am thy servant; give me understanding, that I may know thy testimonies. (Psalms 119:125) Let my cry come near before thee, O Lord: give me understanding according to thy word. (Psalm 119:169)

When we apply wisdom and understanding to all areas of our lives, we will be exceedingly blessed.

Happy is the man who finds wisdom, And the man who gains understanding; For her proceeds are better than the profits of silver,

And her gain than fine gold.
She is more precious than rubies,
And all the things you may desire cannot
compare with her.
Length of days is in her right hand,
In her left hand riches and honor.
Her ways are ways of pleasantness,
And all her paths are peace.
She is a tree of life to those who take hold of her,
And happy are all who retain her.
(Proverbs 3:13-18 NKJV)

Wait on the Lord

Once we learn to pray about everything, we must learn to *wait* on God. I know *waiting* is not a popular option today. However, *waiting on God* is very important in decision making. When we seek God for guidance, He does not always answer us promptly. Sometimes He wants us to wait on Him. I know it is not always easy to wait on the Lord, especially when you have been waiting for a long time. However, the Bible encourages us to wait on the Lord and be of good courage (Psalm 27:14). We do not have to fret or fear when we wait on the Lord. He will strengthen our hearts and answer us.

It is necessary that we learn to wait *patiently* for Him. Do not be in a rush to make a decision once you have prayed. David said, "I waited patiently for the LORD; and he inclined unto me, and heard my cry. He brought me up also out of a horrible pit...and set my feet upon a rock and established my goings. And he hath put a new song in my mouth, even praise unto our God: many shall see it, and fear, and shall trust in the LORD" (Psalm 40:1-3).

In other words, David had to diligently wait on God to free him from a horrible situation in his life. Although waiting on God was not easy for him—he shed some tears along the journey— David endured, and later experienced a mighty deliverance. As a result of waiting on the Lord, David gained stability in his life, a new song and a new praise.

Do you want freedom like that? You can receive it if you patiently wait on the Lord. He has heard your prayers and seen your tears. He is able to bring you out of your horrible pit. And in His own time, He will deliver you from your situation with His strong hand (Psalm 89:13). And when He does, He will give you a new song and a new praise too. Get ready for people to see and trust in your God!

Let us also rest in the Lord *without complaining*. It takes more energy to complain than it does to rejoice. In all honesty, we can all find something to murmur and complain about. The two actions do not change our situations. They only make us feel worse. Try resting in the truth that God knows all about our cases. He also knows how overwhelmed and frustrated we are. We can relax with Him and wait for Him to turn our situations around!

We must also wait *solely* on Him. There are some problems and questions in life that only God can solve and answer. No one on Earth can act on our account like Jesus. We do not need to place our confidence in anyone else but Him. The arms of flesh will fail us. But in God, there is no failure. There is no one like Him or that even compares to Him on the planet. He is the wisest, richest, and most powerful source on Earth and in Heaven.

Put your trust in Him ONLY and expect Him to come through for you. He has not forgotten you. Take comfort in the fact that He is moving on your behalf! And He is capable of bringing to pass every prophetic word spoken over your life.

David said, "My soul, wait thou only upon God; for my expectation is from him" (Psalm 62:5).

Moreover, we must wait with *expectation*. We do not have to wait to praise Him and worship Him until we receive the promise, answer, or direction. We can give Him thanks in advance, knowing at the end, we will receive just what we expected! We know our prayers will come to pass if we pray in His will.

This is the confidence we have in approaching God: that if we ask anything according to his will, he hears us. And if we know that he hears us—whatever we ask—we know that we have what we asked of him. (I John 5:14, 15 NIV)

Finally, let us *continually* wait on the Lord. We should not put a time limit on God, or on how long we will wait on Him. I know it is hard to wait on God when you have been praying for years about something. But if we place our hope in God and His Word, we will not be disappointed or ashamed!

Yea, let none that wait on thee be ashamed: let them be ashamed which transgress without cause. (Psalm 25:3)

We will constantly be faced with choices. Therefore, we must continually pray for His direction, and wait on Him to respond. Do not miss His signals. His GPS system (God's Prayer Signal) is the best in the world!

I am reminded of a song I heard in church years ago. I do not hear people singing it too often today. The words of the song went like this:

> Don't stop praying, the Lord is nigh.
> Don't stop praying, He'll hear your cry.
> The Lord has promised; His word is true.
> Don't stop praying, He'll answer you.

The old saints would get happy when they had sung that song. They knew God answered prayer because they had history with Him—rich and powerful testimonies of healing and deliverance. I believe the song not only blessed others who heard it but blessed the old saints as well. It reminded them of the faithfulness of God.

I am learning how crucial it is to acknowledge God in ALL your decisions, especially the major ones. As I practice to pray about everything, I realize how less stressful life becomes.

I can remember praying diligently about the purchase of my first home. One day, I was sitting in my office at work and God spoke to my heart and said, "Buy a house; I am not bound by your lack of finances." Because I had never owned a house before, I was a little nervous about making this kind of major investment. I knew I needed God's guidance on how, what, when and where to purchase. As I began to pray about this huge undertaking, the Lord began to direct my steps in the process.

I can remember mentioning to a good friend about my decision to buy a house, and she immediately convinced me to talk to her brother who was a mortgage loan officer. She told me her brother would be very helpful in guiding me through the process. After speaking with him, I felt confident about my decision to be a home owner.

As I was praying, I felt prompted by the Holy Spirit to search for a two-bedroom condo. Although one-bedroom condos were more in my price range than two-bedroom condos, I knew God wanted me to trust Him in supplying the financial provision to acquire this type of condo.

Before my purchase, my sister and I discussed living together since her lease was expiring, and I really did not want to live alone. After a few discussions, we decided to be roommates.

The idea of owning a two-bedroom condo was no longer an option for me, but a necessity. My challenge was finding one in a good, affordable neighborhood.

I remember finding a condo and almost purchasing it. The condo was immaculately kept and located in a decent neighborhood. However, it lacked a few things on my wish list.

When I shared the news with a friend, particularly what the condo lacked, he asked me why I was settling to buy something I was not totally satisfied with. The word "settling" really resonated with me. Because I could not see myself investing in property I was not fully content with, I decided not to proceed with the deal.

Finally, I received a call from another realtor regarding some property that contained all the items I desired in my house and more. The only problem was its location. The house was not in the town I anticipated. Even though I was not thrilled about its location, I was curious to check it out.

Before I saw this house, I prayed for God to *order my steps*. I really needed clarity from God if this was indeed the right time to buy property. When I walked in the place, I felt a peace in my spirit and heart to purchase this particular condo.

God had truly exceeded my expectations because the condo contained all my desired items and more. I was so grateful I allowed Him to completely guide me in the process of purchasing my first home.

I realized through this experience, timing is everything. When you pray for His will, pray also for His timing. It was not only His will for me to purchase a home, but His time as well.

Sometimes God blesses us with things we may not initially want. I discovered through this experience, He likes to bless us in measures we least expect. I would have never imagined buying a house in that neighborhood. However, it was a good decision. This is why it is important to pray about everything. God never falls short of knowing what is best for us and how to please us.

I also learned God provides resources for the choices He makes for our lives. He connected me to the right people at the right time to follow the right plan for my life to purchase a home.

He also made provision for me to purchase. I will let you in on a secret: I did not have a great deal of money to purchase a house. Just a WORD and a WILL from God. Standing on His promises and getting in position to receive my blessing activated Heaven to work on my behalf.

Lastly, I was determined to follow His lead no matter what! Even when things looked dim on the surface for me to obtain the house, I maintained my confidence in God and His ability to do the impossible. As a result, God gave me a tailor-made blessing at the appropriate time. Hallelujah!!!!! I would have missed God's best for me had I not acknowledged Him to *order my steps* in this important decision.

Life Application

Key Verse:

"Commit everything you do to the Lord. Trust Him to help you do it, and He will." (Psalm 37:5 TLB)

Personal Reflection:
(1) Do I seek God *daily* for guidance in my life?
(2) Does my *worship* empower me to take *everything to God in prayer?*
(3) Am I praying for His *divine will* and seeking His *wise counsel* in all areas of my life?
(4) Do I wait *patiently, solely, continually,* and with *expectation* on Him to guide me?

Prayer Focus:
Father, I worship You today as *El Elyon,* the Most High God. There is no one like You. My soul will continually seek You, especially in decision making. Equip me in Your presence to acknowledge You in all my ways. Please grant me Your wisdom and understanding in all I say and do. I desire Your divine will for my life. Help me to wait patiently for You, and solely on You to order my steps. I am certain You will answer me at the appointed time. In Jesus' name I pray, Amen!

Follow His Lead

"...And He shall direct your paths."

(Proverbs 3:6 NKJV)

KEY FOUR

The final key I would like to mention is preeminent in making effective decisions. When we take heed to Solomon's wise counsel, outlined in Proverbs 3, verses five and six, and apply it to our lives, we are guaranteed successful results. This proverb gives us a divine assurance that *God will direct our paths.* What a precious promise! It is exciting knowing that when we do our part, God will always do His part. Hallelujah!!!

Throughout the course of history, God proves His faithfulness in keeping His promises to His children. The promises of God are much better than promissory notes because they are

ETERNALLY BINDING. In other words, they are good in this lifetime and throughout eternity.

Unfortunately, we are not like God. Sometimes we keep the promises we make to others and sometimes we do not. Some of our reasons for not following through on our word are justifiable while some are not. Sometimes we just lack integrity. I have never seen a time when people's word meant nothing. I was always taught your word is your bond. If you cannot make good on it, say something. Do not leave people hanging. Thank God we have a Heavenly Father who stays true to every promise written in His Word. His promises may not be fulfilled in our timing, but they are always on schedule according to His timing.

For all of God's promises have been fulfilled in Christ with a resounding "Yes!" And through Christ, our "Amen" (which means "Yes") ascends to God for his glory.
(2 Corinthians 1:20 NLT)

In the Bible, David states that God will guide the steps of the righteous. As we delight in doing His will and consider Him in all our actions, God is pleased and pours blessings our way.

The steps of a good man are ordered by the LORD:
and he delighteth in his way. (Psalm 37:23)

I love this verse! It is comforting to know that nothing happens to a "good man" by coincidence, but by divine order. Every step a *righteous* man takes on the pathway of life is orchestrated by God. God finds enjoyment in keeping the *righteous* safe; making the *righteous* prosper; calming the *righteous'* fears; providing for the *righteous;* and giving the *righteous* peace.

In order to be "good" in God's eyes, we must invite Jesus into our hearts and follow His laws and precepts. Because our righteousness is described as "filthy rags," we are not good on our own merit (Isaiah 64:6). The only way a person can be "right with God" is through Jesus Christ. He paid the price on the cross at Calvary for our sins. We can be justified by God and receive salvation from sin through Jesus. All we have to do is *confess our sins* to Him. He is faithful and just to forgive us our sins and to cleanse us from all wickedness (I John 1:9 NLT).

That if thou shalt confess with thy mouth the Lord
Jesus, and shalt believe in thine heart that God
hath raised him from the dead, thou shalt be

saved. For with the heart man believeth unto righteousness; and with the mouth confession is made unto salvation. (Romans 10:9, 10)

Commit your life to Jesus today so your steps can be *ordered by the Lord.*

When we practice pleasing God and making Him Lord over our lives, our steps will flourish and our way will prosper. Being in "right standing with God" always brings us favor with God. Likewise, we feel good when we are "doing the right thing." Knowing our lives are being guided by an all-knowing and all-powerful God is security at its best!

God also promises to make our lives less burdensome when we follow Him. Jesus said:

"Come to Me, all you who labor and are heavy laden, and I will give you rest. Take My yoke upon you and learn from Me, for I am gentle and lowly in heart, and you will find rest for your souls. For My yoke is easy and My burden is light." (Matthew 11:28 NKJV)

Let Jesus carry your burdens, no matter if they are light or heavy in nature. Life is less stressful when you allow Him to bear your load. You will find the peace and rest your soul desires when you learn to roll your cares over to Him and leave them with Him.

As we continue to stay connected to the One who is good, through our relationship with Jesus Christ, we will grow in righteousness and experience an abundance of blessings as illustrated in this psalm:

Praise the Lord! For all who fear God and trust in him are blessed beyond expression. Yes, happy is the man who delights in doing his commands.

His children shall be honored everywhere, for good men's sons have a special heritage. He himself shall be wealthy, and his good deeds will never be forgotten. When darkness overtakes him, light will come bursting in. He is kind and merciful—and all goes well for the generous man who conducts his business fairly.

Such a man will not be overthrown by evil circumstances. God's constant care of him will make a deep impression on all who see it. He does not fear bad news, nor live in dread of what may happen. For he is settled in his mind that Jehovah will take care of him. That is why he is not afraid but can calmly face his foes. He gives generously to those in need. His deeds will never be forgotten. He shall have influence and honor. (Psalm 112: 1-9 TLB)

Spend Time with God

I have discovered in my walk with God that He speaks regularly to us! The question is "Are we taking time to listen to what He has to say?" God desires to point us in the right direction; however, we must be willing to listen to Him. If we want to know what God has to say about our present and future, we must spend time with Him.

In order to develop intimacy with God, we must have some quality fellowship with Him. I heard Bishop T.D. Jakes say in his sermon entitled, "Intimacy" that Intimacy means "In-To-Me-See." When we are intimate with God, we see Him clearly. We perceive His love for us, His care for us, and His will for us. We also see Him by faith at work in us.

Being filled with Heaven's best is a process that requires time in God's presence. When we take time each day to be alone with God, we will experience an overflow of His love, peace, joy, wisdom, faith, hope, kindness, goodness and abundance.

Being in God's presence also gives you a glimpse of His glory. God's glory is His entire splendor and radiance. As you come into God's presence and focus solely on Him, you will see the beauty of His character and might. Beholding God's glory on any level, gives one the courage and strength to place his or her complete trust in Him.

Spending time with God also empowers you to get things accomplished in your life and for His Kingdom. You will gain confidence in Him and say, like the Apostle Paul, "I can do all things through Christ which strengtheneth me" (Philippians 4:13). In addition, we get a vision of ourselves when we stay at His feet. Sometimes we need God to point out things in our lives that displease Him. When we are in God's presence, He shows us the condition of our hearts and unpleasant attitudes towards others. Repentance is needed if our hearts and attitudes are not right. None of us can afford to lose out with God because of an unclean heart and a bad attitude. Staying in His presence helps to keep our hearts pure and our attitudes in check.

David found being in God's presence a gratifying experience. He states in Psalm 16:11 (WEB), "You will show me the path of life. In your presence is fullness of joy. In your right hand there are pleasures forevermore."

David describes being in God's presence as a pathway to freedom. It leads to complete joy! What a phenomenal feeling...there is nothing in the world like it! Being in His presence brings us sheer delight because of the eternal pleasures it offers us. *Peace* regarding any issue in our lives is one pleasure met in God's presence.

Take time out of your busy schedule and get alone with God. Begin your mornings with Him. David said, "In the morning, O LORD, You will hear my voice; In the morning I will prepare [a prayer and a sacrifice] for You and watch and wait [for You to speak to my heart]" (Psalm 5:3 AMP). God wants to meet you at a time when you are most alert and attentive. Hearing from God requires us to take time out and give Him our undivided attention. I know our time is important to us. It is a very precious commodity. We use it for so many things.

We must be careful not to use all or most of our time giving into our fleshly desires and not building up our spirit man. What we feed the most in our spirits will have the most influence on us. Instead of spending so much time in front of the television, we should spend some quality time "getting to know" God. God wants to help us learn from our past, appreciate and celebrate our present, and plan with anticipation our future. However, He needs time with us to liberate and heal us from our past and present hurts. As we continue to make time for Him, we will experience freedom and healing in our lives.

He cannot disclose to us some of the great plans He has for us if we are not in His presence. It is hard to hear from God if we are not still. Sometimes we are too busy doing things God has not sanctioned us to do.

Just because you are engaged in church work, does not mean you are spending your time wisely for God and with God. Could you possibly be in the wrong position at the wrong time, following the wrong plan for your life? If you are not producing fruit from your labor, you may be out of His will. Doing Kingdom work at the appropriate time is crucial. God knows the right time and the right people to gather the harvest. If you are out of position, you could miss the opportunity to harvest a great number of souls into His Kingdom or forfeit the opportunity to make a difference in someone's life. Therefore, it is imperative to stay close to God so you can fulfill His purpose for your life.

Hear His Voice

God is constantly looking for opportunities to communicate with us. Therefore, it is beneficial for us to hear His voice or pay attention to His cues.

Even in prayer, God desires to speak to us. Are you doing all the talking when you pray? If so, give Him some time to speak. You will be amazed at how much He has to say.

Listening to God requires faith. Faith without works is dead (James 2:26). In other words, you must have faith in hearing His voice. And you must activate your faith in following His lead.

You may not recognize His voice initially; however, the more you yield to it, the more you will become familiar with it. It is just like answering the phone. The more you answer it and listen to the caller's voice, the more familiar you will be with the caller's voice. God is constantly calling us. Are you answering His call? Do you recognize His voice?

You must also learn to distinguish His voice from other voices speaking to you. Your flesh constantly speaks to you. It loves to influence your thinking and dictate your steps. Your flesh is regularly leading you to do things that satisfy your human desires. Remember, your flesh DOES NOT want to please God. It has been tainted by sin and has a sinful nature. Make sure you ask God to help you identify the leading of your flesh or the leading of His Spirit.

Another voice that speaks to us is Satan. Satan loves to persuade our thoughts and actions. He constantly speaks lies to us about ourselves, others and God. We must recognize his voice, especially during times of vulnerability and discouragement. He loves to deceive us and bring confusion to our lives. The Bible refers to him as "the father of lies" (John 8:44 NIV). His primary role is to steer us down a road which leads to eternal damnation. He will not inspire us to do anything good for others or God. He LOVES to send torment our way. He is NOT OUR FRIEND. His highest pleasure is seeing us live defeated lives as Christians.

If you are troubled in your spirit by an action or choice you have made, chances are, you are not being led by His Spirit. God is not the author of confusion, but of peace (1 Corinthians 14:33).

When we make a conscious effort to listen to God, we will hear Him. Generally, He does not speak to us in an audible voice, but He will make Himself known to us. More often, God will speak to our hearts regarding a matter through the prompting of the Holy Spirit. His Spirit will change our hearts and minds regarding people and circumstances when we pray in His will.

God also speaks to us through circumstances. Because I firmly believe nothing happens to us without God's permission, I am learning not to fret about things out of my control. God has taught me over the years, WHEN THINGS ARE OUT OF YOUR CONTROL, HE IS IN CONTROL. And if God is in control, He is working out a far better plan for us than we could ever do for ourselves. God uses circumstances to perfect things in our lives. Let God speak to you through your circumstances.

God also communicates to us through signs and dreams. Many people ask God for signs. If we ask Him for a sign, God will give us a sign. We should look for the sign when we ask Him and ask God to help us recognize it. Do not be guilty of ignoring the sign or signs. If we go past the stop sign or signs He gives us, we may live to regret it.

Moreover, pay attention to your dreams. I have learned to listen to God through dreams. God dealt with people in the Bible through dreams. Remember the wise men that came to worship baby Jesus? They were warned in a dream not to tell King Herod about the baby's whereabouts. They did not know King Herod wanted baby Jesus dead. However, God instructed them in a dream to return to their homeland and not Jerusalem, where King Herod lived. Thank God, they listened to His voice in their dream and obeyed (Matthew 2:1-12).

If you *really* want to hear from God, just read and study the Bible. God will generally reveal His will to you through the Word of God. His guidance never contradicts the Bible.

David describes the Word of God in Psalm 119 as "a lamp unto my feet, and a light unto my path" (Verse 105). Lamps provide light in the midst of darkness. The world is filled with darkness. The Bible describes the way of the wicked like total darkness (Proverbs 4:19 NLT). Being influenced by the world's system and philosophies will place you on a dark track. The end of that track is death.

There is a way which seems right to a man, but in the end it leads to death.
(Proverbs 16:25 WEB)

When we are transformed by God's Word, He directs us onto a path which leads to eternal life. God gave us the Bible to shed light on our journey. Use the Word of God to show you the path, especially when it is cloudy and dark.

I have received so much from God by reading His Word. God will definitely speak to you through His Word if you take time to study it. Many times, I have been led to read something in the Bible that dealt directly with my situation. I knew God was shedding light on something He wanted me to know.

You can find an answer in His Word to any issue you face. Just take the time to find it, read it and reflect on it.

Sometimes, God uses individuals to articulate what He wants us to know. This is one reason why He established the role of pastors in churches. They are God's shepherds to guide His sheep (The congregants). We should listen to them and follow their lead as long as they are following Christ and speak His truth.

Then I will give you shepherds after my own heart, who will lead you with knowledge and understanding. (Jeremiah 3:15 NIV)

I have been blessed to have good shepherds in my life who have given me good leadership. I know God has spoken to me through them on many occasions. My father, the late Bishop Kenneth O. Robinson, Sr., has shepherded me for most of my life. His messages have contributed significantly to my spiritual development. My previous pastor, Elder Donnell Harper, has greatly influenced me in impacting others for the Kingdom of God. The Rev. Gilbert Pickett, Sr., my current shepherd, keeps me reassured and focused, through his anointed and prophetic messages, on the great destiny God has for me.

God also communicates to us through godly men and women. I have been richly blessed by the ministry of various televangelists. Some of my favorites are Bishop T. D. Jakes, Steven Furtick, Jentezen Franklin and Joel Osteen. On several occasions, God has used them to directly speak to me. I can remember Joel Osteen preaching a message regarding peace. It was a timely message for me because I was struggling with peace in my life. I knew God was telling me through His manservant to choose His peace and dismiss the devil's distress. That evening, I heard a life changing word from God. I was liberated in my mind by making a conscious effort to receive God's peace in my heart and release the enemy's anxiety over my life. Praise God!

Rely on the Holy Spirit

In one of my previous chapters, I talked about *unseen realities*. The *Holy Spirit* is another unseen reality operating in the world and in us to control our actions and paths. Although we cannot see Him, we know He exists. We can feel or sense His presence when we take the time to acknowledge Him. He is One who cannot be ignored or left out of any decision or situation in our lives.

It is through the Holy Spirit that the Word of God is applied to our hearts and new life in Christ is acquired. Without the Holy Spirit, we would not desire God or be a part of His family. He is the

One who draws men and women to Christ (John 6:44). His abiding presence is always with those who follow Christ. Although we cannot see God, we can feel Him through the Holy Spirit.

He is considered the third person in the Godhead—God the Father, God the Son and *God the Holy Spirit*. He worked in conjunction with God and His son, Jesus, when man was created.

And God said, Let us make man in our image, after our likeness: and let them have dominion over the fish of the sea, and over the fowl of the air, and over the cattle, and over all the earth, and over every creeping thing that creepeth upon the earth. (Genesis 1:26)

Before Jesus ascended to His Father after His resurrection, He told His disciples He was sending them additional help in the form of the Holy Spirit.

And I will pray the Father, and he shall give you another Comforter, that he may abide with you forever; (John 14:16)

But the Comforter, which is the Holy Ghost, whom the Father will send in my name, he shall teach you all things, and bring all things to your remembrance, whatsoever I have said unto you. (John 14:26)

However when he, the Spirit of truth, has come, he will guide you into all truth, for he will not speak from himself; but whatever he hears, he will speak. He will declare to you things that are coming. (John 16:13 WEB)

But ye shall receive power, after that the Holy Ghost is come upon you: and ye shall be witnesses unto me both in Jerusalem, and in all Judaea, and in Samaria, and unto the uttermost part of the earth. (Acts 1:8)

Jesus knew He would be leaving His disciples shortly and that they needed a similar source like Him, to help them carry out the mission of the church and to do great exploits for His Kingdom. This is why He promised to send them another Comforter, the Holy Spirit, who would lead them into all truth by illuminating their minds in the Word and empowering them to be witnesses for Him.

He is the *Paracletes*, a Greek term for Comforter, which means, "One called alongside to help." His role is to guide us along life's journey; convict us of our sins; empower us for daily living; and bring all things to our remembrance, when necessary. If we let Him, He will do magnificent things in our lives and through our lives. It is through Him that we live and we move, and we have our being (Acts 17:28).

He abides in our hearts to help us in making the right choices for our lives. He also enables us to surrender our will to God. The Bible teaches us "if we live in the spirit, let us also walk in the spirit" (Galatians 5:25). In other words, if we profess to possess the Spirit, then we should follow His lead.

When we observe men and women in the Bible that were led by the Spirit in making decisions, they were immensely blessed. Esther is a woman who was led by the Spirit in saving her nation, Israel, from annihilation. Being strategically placed in Persia due to exile, Esther found favor in the King's eyes when she was chosen amongst the other women in the palace to be his next queen. She was in the right place at the right time to help her people. When Esther heard through her uncle, Mordecai, Haman's plan to destroy all the Jews, she immediately sought God. She relied on the Holy Spirit to give her an answer to the Jews' dilemma.

Esther led her people to fast and pray with sackcloth and ashes for three days. Sackcloth and ashes were used in those days in times of national disaster and/or for repentance of sin. The Jews intensely mourned and distressed over the devastating news regarding their race. They fasted, wept and wailed before God to deliver them from this horrible fate. As a result of their actions, God revealed to Esther a strategy to save her people. Although it was a risky undertaking: going before the King, Esther gained courage and strength to approach him through the spiritual weapons of fasting and prayer. She did not mind implementing the plan, even if it meant losing her own life in the process.

And Mordecai told them to answer Esther: "Do not think in your heart that you will escape in the king's palace any more than all the other Jews. For if you remain completely silent at this time, relief and deliverance will arise for the Jews from another place, but you and your father's house will perish. Yet who knows whether you have come to the kingdom for such a time as this?"

Then Esther told them to reply to Mordecai: "Go, gather all the Jews who are present in Shushan, and fast for me; neither eat nor drink for three days, night or day. My maids and I will fast likewise. And so I will go to the king, which is against the law; and if I perish, I perish!"
(Esther 4:13-16 NKJV)

By following the Holy Spirit, Esther and the people witnessed a great victory. God reversed the decree of death against the Jews and Haman was hung instead (Esther 7-9).

Esther and the Jews would have never received their breakthrough without relying on the Holy Spirit for a solution to their crisis. If we lean on the Spirit to give us answers to our issues, we will experience similar breakthroughs.

The Holy Spirit wants to have a relationship with us. He is constantly tugging at our hearts to help us and guide us. Do you feel His prompting? He can do marvelous things for us, in us and through us if we cultivate a relationship with Him. Depend on Him today to lead you down the road to victory for you and your family.

Sometimes He chooses a path for us that goes against our wills or detours us from the road we are currently on. Even though we may not like or understand His choice for us, we must trust Him. He knows what He is doing. He has a proven track record of performing the AMAZING in the lives of those who allow Him to.

Obey Him

It is imperative that we obey God as He directs our path. God honors obedience. It is our highest calling to Him. Jesus told His disciples, "If you [really] love Me, you will keep and obey My commandments" (John 14:15 AMP). In other words, Jesus challenged His disciples to prove their love for Him by their obedience to Him. We may proclaim our love for God; however, it means nothing, if we do not obey Him. We show Him how much we love Him by how much we obey Him. When we obey His Word and love our fellow brother, God is pleased.

Even our sacrifices do not weigh much to God when we do not obey Him. God rejected Saul as King of Israel and his sacrifice to Him because of his disobedience. Instead of utterly destroying the Amalekites and all their possessions like God commanded, Saul decided to save the best of their sheep, oxen and fatling and sacrifice it to the Lord. The Lord was not pleased with Saul's decision to deviate from His instructions, and told him "...Behold, to obey is better than sacrifice, and to hearken than the fat of rams" (1 Samuel 15:1-22).

God cares more about your obedience to Him than any sacrifice you can make to Him. If you offer the sacrifice of praise and worship to Him and walk in disobedience, it is not a sweet-smelling savor to Him. Do you know obedience is a form of worship? God does not receive your adoration if your heart is disobedient towards Him.

He is also not impressed with your sacrificial giving. It is nice to be charitable and give to the church and others. However, your giving does not earn you brownie points with God when you live disobedient to His Word. You will be blessed when you give because of the principle of giving, "Give and it will be given to you: good measure, pressed down, shaken together, and running over will be put into your bosom" (Luke 6:38 NKJV). However, your giving will not guarantee you eternal life if you do not obey Him.

As God directs our paths, let us follow His lead. We will never regret following God's path; only gain. Some of us will never know how blessed our lives could be until we obey Him. I strongly believe obedience is the key to "abundant living."

Maybe God is leading you to do something you feel uncomfortable doing or do not want to do. Or maybe He is directing you do to something you feel inadequate doing. My advice to you, just do it. As you take one step towards obeying Him, He will meet you and help you make the second, third, and fourth step. He knows every concern you have towards not following His lead.

Sometimes our disobedience is due to fear. Whatever it is, we can express it to God and He will give us the boldness and strength to walk in His way for our lives.

What good is it to receive instruction from someone and not follow it? Let us not be guilty of ignoring God's instruction for our lives. Regardless of our opinion of it, let us trust His leadership. He is far more capable of leading us to victory than we are of leading ourselves. If we follow His lead, we will be *more than conquerors* in any situation.

As we see in the story of Esther, victory is always gained when you obey God. Obedience means everything to Him. Ask Adam and Eve.

They lost everything in the Garden because of disobedience: their position, and fellowship and relationship with God. Because of Adam's disobedience, sin entered into the world resulting in condemnation for all men. However, because of the obedience of Jesus Christ, all men have the opportunity to be justified for their sins through faith in His redemptive work on the cross. Through Christ, we can receive a new relationship with God, a rich fellowship with Him and one day, eternal life with God.

Therefore, as through one man's offense judgment came to all men, resulting in condemnation, even so through one Man's righteous act the free gift came to all men, resulting in justification of life. For as by one man's disobedience many were made sinners, so also by one Man's obedience many will be made righteous. (Romans 5:18, 19 NKJV)

I am reminded of a testimony told to me by a friend. One day her church decided to embark on a project to build a new facility. They wanted to build in a certain area of town. They had specific floor plans drawn for their desired new facility. The church spent several years working with the city in building new construction and raising funds for their building project. One day, the city asked them for an additional $20,000 towards the project. After much prayer, her pastor felt prompted by the Spirit not to give the city what they asked for. Instead, he continued to pray for direction on how to proceed with this project.

A few months later, a pastor from the area, called him and said he had a church building for rent. Apparently, his church was no longer able to keep up the building and was looking to rent it to another church.

When her pastor saw the inside of the church, he found its floor plan similar to the floor plan they desired in their new building. He knew this opportunity to rent this church building was a blessing from God.

Had her pastor not followed the leading of the Spirit and given the city additional funds; the church would not have had the money to rent and beautify their new building. God provided for them another church facility without going through the headache of building a new construction. What a magnificent God we serve! He is truly devoted to those who trust and OBEY Him!

∽

Following God's lead always pays off. It takes, however, a great deal of discipline. Exercising discipline to develop a sensitive ear to consistently hear what the Spirit is saying and leading you to do is a process. If you are willing to trust Him to guide you every step along the journey, even when you do not know where He is directing you, you will have a bountiful end.

Through the years, I have learned and I might add, am still learning, to follow His lead. It has not always been a smooth path, but I have discovered it is a rewarding one. Even when it came to writing this book, I had to learn to follow His lead. Sixteen years ago, God challenged me to write this book. At first, I did not follow His lead because of fear. I lacked confidence in my ability to write a book. However, I could not rest in my spirit until I was obedient in fulfilling His will for my life. When I finally said, "yes" to God and followed His lead, He directed my path and gave me the grace I needed to complete this project.

Sometimes you may not know why He is leading you down a particular pathway. This was certainly my case when I was called to the ministry. In my early years of ministry, I did not feel very adequate in preaching His Word to others. However, what I discovered from my call to ministry was "who God calls, He equips." He is more concerned with our *availability* than our ability. All we have to do is say, "yes" and He will qualify us.

During the early years of my calling, God revealed to me that my focus in ministry should be helping others get through hurt and pain in their lives. There are many people hurting in the world and in the church. God calls individuals in this area of ministry to meet the needs of people who need some sort of freedom in their lives. This could range from childhood hurt to adult abuse. You could even experience a church hurt that cripples you mentally and spiritually in working for the Kingdom of God.

I was shocked God wanted to use me in this area of ministry since I struggled with being delivered in some areas of my life. God showed me, however, that ministries are birthed out of our painful experiences and struggles. Having struggled with my own fears and insecurities, I truly desired to see others freed from these struggles as well.

In my early years of ministry, my messages were centered when prompted by the Spirit towards helping others find freedom in their lives. Although my knowledge in this area of ministry was limited, the one thing I was certain about due to my own personal experience was: GOD WILL LIBERATE YOU IF YOU WANT TO BE FREE. The more I pursued deliverance in certain areas of my life, the more I experienced it from God.

There was a season in my life when God was not using me as often in this area of ministry. Although I knew God had chosen me to help others through my calling, I felt He had placed me on hold for the time being.

During this season, God began to order my steps into a deeper prayer life. When my mother took seriously ill in 2007, God used her illness to draw me closer to Him through prayer. I was also asked to join an intercessory prayer ministry led by a very close friend, which met early in the morning on a conference line to pray. Even though getting up at 5:00 a.m. to pray was a challenge, I graciously consented because I knew God had called me to be an intercessor.

Through this prayer ministry, currently known as ETPIM Global (End-Time Prophetic Intercession Ministries), and founded by Pastor

Mireille Desrosiers, I learned the importance of prayer, the power of prayer, and how-to pray effectively in order to get results. My exposure to this realm of prayer made a tremendous difference in my life and ministry.

In addition, after serving as a school counselor for eight years, God ordered my steps into the mental health profession. Initially, I was not passionate about this area of counseling. It was never my desire to obtain my professional license as a mental health counselor. However, I have learned over the years not to question the Spirit's leading, but to simply obey Him. I knew I would understand it better in the future.

The more I studied mental health, the more I became interested in this field of counseling. I particularly found my clinical internship exciting and fulfilling.

One day, God told me that I had come full circle with His plan for my life. He showed me how He had been ordering my steps all along in the ministry of helping others. It was in those silent years of ministry that God was perfecting my calling in my life. By following His leadership, I learned that it takes Bible study, prayer, and counseling to experience deliverance in your life.

I realized He had strategically guided me into a prayer ministry that would teach me all the things I need to know about prayer and its role in helping others. It was through the powerful intercessory prayer ministry, ETPIM Global that I reached a level of prayer that I needed for the call on my life. Through ETPIM Global, I learned you must have a prayer life and understand the power of prayer when assisting others to find deliverance in their lives.

He had also purposefully led me down the road of mental health counseling. He revealed to me how counseling plays a key role in helping a person acquire freedom from past and present hurts. People need to acknowledge and talk about their pain with a professional in order to be liberated from certain chains in their lives that have them bound. God was broadening my knowledge base and sharpening my skills as a counselor so I could incorporate them into my ministry. I knew how to counsel teens through school counseling. I gained experience counseling adults through mental health counseling. What a mighty God we serve!

From the time He revealed to me His plan for my life, until the present, God was orchestrating my steps and directing my path in this call of ministry. Thank God, I followed His direction! Even when I did not understand what He was doing in my life and why He was leading me down certain paths like ETPIM and the mental health profession, I am glad I obeyed Him. Had I not obeyed Him and pursued the paths He laid out for me, I would not be as equipped as I am today spiritually and professionally.

Today, I am a student at New York Theological Seminary pursuing my latest calling—a chaplain. When God first directed my steps towards seminary, I was a little nervous, not fully understanding why God was leading me to study theology at this stage in my life, and not fully aware of the many opportunities that will be afforded to me outside the church setting with a seminary education. However, as I continued to follow God's lead on this journey, I became more cognizant of His will for me in seminary and for the future. One thing I discovered was that my mental health training was all a part of God's plan for me to become a chaplain. My background in mental health is valuable in this call of ministry and will enhance my effectiveness as a chaplain. I am excited about becoming a chaplain because it is another opportunity for me to help people but at a larger scale and scope. Likewise, chaplaincy is another dimension in the area of ministry God has called me to serve.

As we can see from my story, we never go wrong when we follow His lead. God always proves faithful in preparing us for the call He has placed on our lives. Not only for our calling, but for any decision we must make for our lives. All we have to do is *trust Him wholeheartedly; not rely on our own intellect; pray about everything;* and most of all, *follow His lead.* When we do these things, we will live exciting and fulfilled lives because we are allowing Him to *order our steps.*

Life Application

~~~

Key Verse:

"The Lord directs our steps, so why try to understand everything along the way?" *(Proverbs 20:24 NLT)*

Personal Reflection:

(1) Am I *standing* on *God's promises* in my life?

(2) How much *quality time* do I really spend with God?

(3) Am I *listening* to Him when He speaks to me?

(4) Do I *recognize* and *follow* the *prompting* of the Holy Spirit in my life?

Prayer Focus:

Lord, You are so awesome! Your promises are astounding! Help me to stand on every promise You have given me in Your Word. I desire to spend more time in Your presence so I can hear from You and enjoy the peace and joy it brings. Free me from distractions that rob my time with You. Let me recognize Your voice when You speak to me and reject all other voices that try to negatively influence me. Please help me to be sensitive to the Spirit so I can follow Your lead. I decree and declare I will walk in full obedience to You and Your Word. In Jesus Name, Amen!

ABOUT THE AUTHOR

Brenda Joyce Robinson is committed to making a positive impact in the lives of others. Her call to ministry began in 1988 at New Covenant Temple United Holy Church, under the pastorate of the late Bishop Kenneth O. Robinson, Sr. As a result of her leadership in various areas of ministry such as youth ministry, music ministry, evangelism, Christian education and women's ministry, Brenda was ordained in 2009 as an Elder by the United Holy Church of America.

Brenda is currently an associate minister at the Mount Horeb Baptist Church, under the leadership of Reverend Gilbert Pickett, Sr. Her love and passion for evangelism inspired her to establish and serve as the ministry leader for MHBC Bread of Life Evangelistic Outreach Ministry.

Brenda is a middle school counselor and a volunteer bereavement counselor in Rockland County, New York. In 2009, Brenda was recognized by the National Sorority of Phi Delta Kappa, Inc., and awarded the Bridge Builder's Award for her outstanding accomplishments in Education, and dedicated service to the youth of Rockland County.

Her strong desire to help the hurting has inspired her to pursue her license as a mental health counselor. As a graduate student of New York Theological Seminary, Brenda's future aspiration is to become a chaplain.

ORDER INFORMATION

You can order additional copies of *Order My Steps* by emailing the author directly using the email address below:

Brenda J. Robinson

Email Address:
brcounselor@yahoo.com

Books are available at Amazon.com, BN.com Kindle and Your Local Bookstores (By Request)

Please leave a review for this book on Amazon and let other readers know how much you enjoyed reading it.

Thank you!

Made in the USA
Middletown, DE
21 June 2019